# intrinsic awakened nature
MANIFEST THE WISDOM OF THE PURE MIND

### Venerable Master Miao Tsan

**bright sky press**
HOUSTON, TEXAS

**bright sky press**
HOUSTON, TEXAS

2365 Rice Boulevard, Suite 202,
Houston, Texas 77005

www.brightskypress.com

Library of Congress Cataloging-in-Publication Data on file with publisher.

Original Zen poetry at chapter open and close © 2012 by Master Miao Tsan
Translated by Jay L. Gao in collaboration
with MasterWord Services, Inc.

10  9  8  7  6  5  4  3  2  1

ISBN 978-1-936474-70-7 (softcover)

Editorial Direction, Lucy Chambers; Creative Direction, Ellen Cregan
Printed in China through Asia Pacific Offset

Master Your Mind.

Master Your Life.

intrinsic awakened nature

# ACKNOWLEDGEMENTS

I would like to acknowledge the following people for their help with *Intrinsic Awakened Nature*. A book is a collaboration of talents, and this one has benefited from the efforts of many dedicated individuals.

Jay L. Gao and Larry Payne, in conjunction with MasterWord Services, Inc. translated the manuscript from Chinese into English. They spent countless hours revisiting the original text to ensure the translation remained true to the original meaning and to express concepts in a clear, consistent manner.

Ludmila and Alexandre Golovine have provided generous support, tireless effort and enthusiasm for this book, as well as for *Just Use This Mind* and *The Origin Is Pure*. Without their wholehearted commitment to this project, these books would not exist in English or Spanish.

At Bright Sky Press, Lucy Chambers edited the translation, and Ellen Cregan and Marla Garcia designed it to make it accessible and beautiful for readers.

Thanks to Nan Ye, Vicky Ong, Olga Daggs, Jennifer Farmer and Adrianne Poyet-Smith at MasterWord Services, Inc. for their tireless work with translation, manuscript and logistical details.

Jui-min Su, Jung-Wei Chen, Eric Sun, Heng-Yin Yang, Naishin Chang and Fernando E. Delfin offered invaluable insights during the editorial process.

Finally, I am grateful to my brother, Dr. Tien-Sheng Hsu, for his support of the original Chinese version of *Instrinsic Awakened Nature* in Taiwan.

Shih, Miao Tsan

# TABLE OF CONTENTS

# PREFACE:
# A LONE BEING AMONG
# THOUSANDS OF APPEARANCES

Lit incense in the open hall startles devils and demons;
Tip of the scepter again presents the Brahman's
flower offering.
The void smashes and three continents scatter,
Whereupon the monk rolls with laughter.

I often have opportunities in the West to have discussions with priests and pastors on the similarities and differences between Western and Eastern religions. For instance, I was invited to attend a seminar that focused on the differences and similarities between these respective theologies and philosophies. There was a poet in the audience. After hearing my speech on the Zen Mind, he recounted the lesson from a lama that if there were truly God there would be no suffering. He was under the impression that the lama was an atheist, and having heard my opinions on the Mind, he believed the same of me.

I explained that the formless, omnipresent and all-powerful God in Western religions—revered as the Creator of everything— is similar to the fundamental principle of the formless, omnipresent Mind in Zen, which gives rise to everything. I suggested that the personality factor, political factor or generational factor blurs their similarities and further exaggerates their differences.

Despite the distinct ways in which they spread their teachings, many Western and Eastern religions share common principles. The Buddha nature, or the Mind, refers to a universal creative process: It creates functions and appearances, but it has neither substance nor form. In this respect, Buddhists are atheistic. In Western religions, the understanding of "God" also refers to the process of creation, except that this function has been expressed as the creation of material things.

Religious Westerners must therefore be cautious in labeling Buddhism as a kind of atheism. The Buddhist teaching that everyone possesses the innate Buddha nature is really another way of saying, "God lives in your heart." The concept that God creates men is very similar to the concept that the Mind creates all phenomena. The glorification of God and the solemn dignity of Pure Land are also similar. It is impossible to compare and contrast various religions in one or two sentences. Highly educated religious thinkers must engage in deep discussion and extensive investigation before any meaningful conclusion can be drawn.

Humanity seeks eternity, happiness and the ability to understand the meaning of life. The goals of these pursuits are consistent with each other. Beneath their differences in ideologies, languages and cultures lie the core values shared by many religions and belief systems. However, most people are perplexed by the differences on the surface and feel conflicted as to which religion or ideology most deserves their loyalty.

It is impossible to completely assimilate the different circumstances of another culture. Any attempt to merge two distinct cultures will, at best, yield a third culture. However different they may seem on the surface, at the source of these cultures lies the one and only Universal Truth.

The Universal Truth, also known as the First Cause and the principle of life, is the original creative force. It includes the operational principle that governs appearances and forms. This truth manifests itself in every situation, but it transcends them all. Once we as human beings master the Universal Truth and its proper application, we can find a solution to end all conflicts. If we understand it and live by it, we will be able to attain a more advanced civilization. A self-centered culture is neither healthy nor complete. Detached from the Universal Truth, the superfluous assimilation of cultures only yields a third culture, a fourth culture and so on. A multidimensional culture is by no means the end of conflict.

Unless it is armed with the goal of teaching the Universal Truth, a religion—no matter the nature of its rituals—will not successfully adapt to the progression of time and generational changes. A religion that transcends time and space is solely devoted to advocating truth. My goal in teaching—and sharing the ideas in this book—is to illuminate others with the Zen understanding of the creative source and driving force behind all appearances in the universe. My mission is to teach others how to experience the Universal Truth and use it to make their lives more fulfilling.

Zen Buddhism, long prevalent in the East, values enlightenment first and foremost. It emphasizes the practitioner's recovery of his own innate Mind. Each of us is born with this innate Mind, and it is the source of life that creates all of our circumstances. All teachings about the Mind explain the existence and functioning principle of creation and elaborate on its implications. Upon enlightenment, the Mind becomes its own master. Active and alert, it demonstrates truth at every moment. The active and lively state of an enlightened mind can be illustrated through the *koans*.

Consider the well-known koan "Master Zhaozhou's encounter with Granny of WuTai Mountain." A monk, on his journey to Mt. WuTai, asked an old woman, "Which is the way to Mt. WuTai?" Granny replied, "Straight ahead," whereupon the monk set forth. Granny said, "Yet another monk who goes like this." The monk later reported this incident to his master, who decided to see for himself. The following day, the master went to the old woman and asked, "Which is the way to Mt. WuTai?" The old woman answered, "Straight ahead," and the master proceeded accordingly. The granny said, "Yet another monk who goes like this." The master returned and told the monk, "I have seen through that Mt. WuTai granny for you."

One either recognizes the truth directly or not; if one reads between the lines and thinks left and right, enlightenment will only elude the pursuer. So, how did Master Zhaozhou see through the old woman? If you can answer this question, you have reached the same level as Master Zhaozhou. Otherwise, let us engage the question for five to ten years and see if we can achieve such a realization.

Zen Buddhism comprises five schools, within which there are seven main lineages. The lineages of Zen teaching are passed from one enlightened person to another, based on the mind-to-mind confirmation of spiritual realization. To obtain enlightenment, a Zen master embarks on a pilgrimage to search for the dharma lineage with which he or she has a karma connection. A lineage is always centered on dharma, the Mind and enlightenment. Unlike most religious sects, which are defined by organizational structures or specific people, the heritage of the ancestral Zen masters is a lineage based on the truth. Another koan, which we will revisit in the last chapter of this book, illustrates the concept of Zen lineage. Master Wenyi had once been a disciple of Master Huilin, but he did not achieve enlightenment under his tutelage. Later, during a pilgrimage, Wenyi achieved enlightenment under the guidance of Master Guichen. When Wenyi started his own teaching, Master Huilin's head monk Zizhao led a group of disciples to question him on whose teaching he had followed.

Wenyi replied that he followed Master Guichen's teaching, but Zizhao became furious and accused Wenyi of betraying Master Huilin's teaching. Wenyi, in response, presented Zizhao with the question he had continually pondered while under the guidance of Master Huilin: "What is 'a lone being among thousands of appearances'?" Zizhao raised the duster, but Wenyi said, "This reply is what you learned from Master Huilin. What about your own reply?" Zizhao was speechless.

Wenyi then asked, "To stand out from thousands of appearances, should one separate from them or not?" Zizhao responded in the negative, but all the other followers responded in the affirmative. Subsequently, after several rounds of debate, Zizhao realized his own flaws. From then on, he practiced under Master Wenyi. He did not establish his own monastery, even after he attained enlightenment.

Genuine seekers gather at one congruous word and part at one incongruous word, focusing on the nature of matters but wasting no words. If asked whose teachings I follow, I would reply that the answer lies in how Master Zhaozhou sees through Granny, of Mt. WuTai, as well as in whom Wenyi follows.

> Saintly or mundane, like iron pegs,
> all must go through the smelting process.
> The transcendence and harmony of enlightenment
> dwarfs the peak of Mt. Hua.

**Miao Tsan**
Vairocana Zen Monastery

# 1 COMING BACK TO LIFE'S LESSONS

Long and short floral branches stretch
into the spring of March;
Chilly mountain spring flows over boulders.
Everlasting illumination, setting sun glows with red;
There is a master behind the flow of yin and yang
and heaven and earth.

## Faithful Perseverance Leads One Back to the Source

The foundation of life is a correct life view, which determines the direction and path we should take. Different life views steer us toward different religious beliefs. Even within the same religious belief, people follow paths toward different destinations, as defined by their life views.

The term "life view" refers to our perspective on life and the attitude with which we live. The key to the mastery of our destiny is to learn how to properly shape our view toward life. Religious belief and practice are inseparable from life view, and therefore life views can be divided into comprehensive ones and limited ones. Those that focus on current social trends are evidently short-sighted and limited, because they are prone to the kinds of changes associated with ethnicities, time, circumstances and cultures.

Comprehensive life views explore the origin of life. Only with a full understanding of the origin of life can anyone experience a life that is happy and perfect. Without such an understanding, we will lead a life of confusion and contradiction.

The process of correcting incorrect views, attitudes and approaches to life is called cultivation. The key element in cultivation is a proper understanding of what life is about, as our life view. If we do not establish a life view centered on an understanding of the source of life, our cultivation could be compared to the work of a headless fly, seemingly busy and diligent but utterly devoid of purpose.

Each of us should set clearly defined goals for cultivation as opposed to going about the effort blindly. Buddhism has temples, scriptures, teachings, monastic and lay practitioners, meditations, chanting and mantra practices. None of these is the goal itself, but each serves certain goals.

What are correct views? From the Christian perspective, the most fundamental view is of God: God is all. God is the Creator; the source of all life. Without God, nothing can be established. In Christianity—as in Judaism and Islam—there are congregations, clergy and holy texts, and their common, clear and powerful goal is to return to God.

Regardless of one's religion or sect, as long as someone has faith in God as the source of life, in the end he will return to the source. When we scrutinize any religion from this perspective, we realize where its flaws and weaknesses lie. From the Western perspective, God is the Creator and the sole source of human happiness, suffering and predicaments. Therefore, practitioners pray to God and feel gratitude toward God. Given the framework in which God has created mankind, it is fruitless for a man to beg for help from his fellow men because they are all created the same way.

Zen Buddhism holds that everyone has the original Mind. When someone is confused, he should turn to the Mind for answers; when faced with difficulty, he should turn to the Mind for solutions. Most people try to resolve one illusory circumstance— or appearance—with another, but it is impossible for one form of attachment to resolve another. We must go back to the source of all appearances and the origin of all life, which is the Mind. The structures of Western religions work together to guide people back to the Creator. Contrastingly, the Zen structures and practice aim people toward understanding the Mind, because it is the source of all thoughts, emotions and occurrences.

Many seekers have studied the Four Noble Truths: suffering, accumulation, cessation and the path of cessation. There are many kinds of suffering in life, including birth, illness, aging, death, parting with beloved ones, encountering grief and resentment, and the anguish of our human condition. Suffering is a result of attachment, or the cumulative pursuit of phenomena from outside the Mind. One thought follows another, and one habit is created after another. In this manner, thoughts and habits are accumulated. If you want to eliminate the problems caused by this accumulation of thoughts and habits, you must apply the appropriate method.

The Four Noble Truths are the fundamentals of Buddhist teachings, but do they mention the source? Without going back to the source, how does anyone achieve enlightenment and nirvana? This is a subtle point. The Four Noble Truths are the core dharma of Buddhism, and as such they equate to the scriptures of other religions such as the Bible, Torah or Quran. It is unfathomable to teach the Bible without referring to God. Without a God-focus, there is no clear source and therefore no motivation to return to the source. In the same way, people who talk about the Four Noble Truths do not necessarily make progress. They need to direct their efforts toward a clear direction of practice and, ultimately, liberation.

It is not wrong to talk about the Twelve Links of dependent origination, the Three Dharma Seals, the contemplation of feelings as suffering and the physical body as impermanence, or to refer to all phenomena as lacking fundamental substance. These concepts are all correct. However, from ancient times till the present, for the countless masters and practitioners who have studied these principles, the real question is whether they have been able to go back to the source and achieve liberation. It is not so easy to do. Buddhists study scriptures the same way Christians study the Bible. A person who studies the Bible without the goal of returning to God may, at best, pick up some ideas about life, but this approach cannot clarify the fundamental purpose of Christianity. Without this larger purpose, cultivation will be confused and the goal of liberation will remain distant.

It is a serious problem when a Buddhist, trapped beneath the weight of vexation, attachment and ignorance, claims a true understanding of the Four Noble Truths and the Twelve Links of dependent origination. All skillful teachings and practices serve one purpose. In Western religions, this purpose is very clear: It is God. Buddhism, however, due to its long history and widespread scriptures, is burdened with many different beliefs and theories, which cloud the core concept of a return to the source of life.

The fundamental purpose of cultivation is to return to the source of life. Consequently, in order to tackle a problem we must find its source and work from there. It does not matter what we say or how we say it, nor does it matter whether one's life aims toward the Paradise of Western religion or the Eastern Pure Land: They are not the source of human issues. Our issues originate in the Mind, which is the Creator or the Source. Reincarnation in some paradise or the Pure Land—the body, function and appearance associated with that reincarnation—is a creation of the Mind. Reincarnation on earth is also a creation of the Mind.

It is critical that we clarify our understanding of the source of life and return to it. It seems many Buddhists work hard all the time with no clear goal, direction or a sense of urgency, because they do not know where the source is. This lack of direction explains their lack of progress.

Does progress mean practicing in a prayer hall that is grander than another, or studying more scriptures? Does praying in a bigger church or with a more sophisticated priest deliver you more quickly back to God? No. Whatever your spiritual practice or ideology is, you can only reach the ultimate goal through the firm faith and consistent cultivation that return you to the source of life.

The goal of Zen study is to learn and practice the truth that the Mind is the source of all appearances; the place where the solutions to all problems can be found. None of us can solve any issue but our own. The proper practice is to understand the Mind, find the Mind, rest in the Mind and cultivate through the Mind.

## The Original Mind Is the Indestructible Eternity

Zen practice emphasizes the realization and recovery of the practitioner's original Mind. It eradicates attachments to reveal the functionality and nature of the Mind. In this way the Mind is like a mirror. An ordinary person's mind is a mirror covered with dust, but an enlightened mind is free of dust. It faithfully reflects the light from the origin. The path to enlightenment lies within, not without. We must reflect, illuminate and transform ourselves from within.

The Eastern realm, the Western realm, the human world, Paradise and hell are not sources of life but are temporary manifestations of it. The Mind is the source of all appearances, functions and existence. Without the Mind, we would not be able to return home. This is equally true from the perspectives of religion, philosophy and practical experience.

Only efforts applied from the Mind can resolve the conflicts, afflictions and problems that arise from duality. Going through the motions of practicing without clear understanding, constant effort and real experience will not lead to true conviction. A person who has this kind of spiritual practice drifts from one idea to another and ultimately sees others as the causes of his own issues.

The predicaments and vexations in life are the work of your mind alone. No one else can or should be responsible for them. What is the true significance of the Buddhist teachings? Buddha does not rescue people, but instead Buddha teaches us to save ourselves. The human mind is capable of functioning just like the Buddha mind. Buddha simply teaches us how to properly use the Mind, which then leads to the desired result. He does not give us the ability to create, nor does he try to resolve our self-inflicted problems.

Buddhist dharma states that because we have the innate Mind and Buddha nature, we must be responsible for all appearances in life; no one else can generate thoughts or create relationships for us. The Mind is yours, and so is your destiny. There is no escape other than self-cultivation and self-liberation.

We must know clearly where to return; where the true refuge of our practice lies. This is not a matter of reincarnation in the Eastern or Western realms, since both are just phenomena created by the Mind. We must return to the true home, the source of life. When a troublesome thought stirs, most people feel distress because they attribute the thought to the creating Mind. However, the thought itself is a creation, so it makes just as much sense to perceive it in another way.

The Creator has a limitless ability to create, but whatever is created is temporary and fleeting. The Mind, in creating, is innate and versatile, so our true self is not just a single thought or body. The Mind creates the myriad past, present and future selves as well as various realms such as those of heaven, the human world, hell, demons and beasts. However, the totality of the appearances thus created does not equate to the Mind.

Look wherever appearances and energy are, and there you will find the functioning of the Mind, encompassing them. The Mind is not just your present body, thoughts and emotions. These relationships and circumstances are only creations of the Mind in the moment. If we are attached to the manifestation of the present moment as our self or ego might identify it, we cannot separate our true selves from the corresponding disease, personality and relations of this identified self.

Our freedom in life becomes very restricted when we equate the Creator to the created appearances, personalities and relations. When we do so, we initiate a vicious cycle of continuously creating identities, diseases and relationships according to our habitual tendencies. You are not who you identify as yourself. Instead, you are the one who created the "you" to which you have become identified. Your thoughts and emotions result from the temporary functions of the Mind, so they are not the true you. You can immediately separate from this self-identity as soon as you realize that your true self is the Mind, which creates all.

Freedom requires that we bring every appearance in life back to its source. A Zen Buddhist must recover his original Mind; otherwise, his practice is little more than a fleeting phenomenon. Some people are very good at meditating for long hours in prayer halls, but they lose momentum soon after they leave the environment of prayer. The mind immediately begins to gather dust again. Some Buddhists practice monasticism and hope to continue doing so in the next life. This is not necessarily possible, however. Death, like any change, is a phenomenon subject to arising and dissolution.

An individual can certainly bring knowledge and views with him to the next life. What Sakyamuni or many past masters have left in their relics are not their physical bodies but knowledge of the Mind attained through their own realization. True knowledge of life starts with enlightenment and cultivation based on the experience of enlightenment. The true eternal relic is not a perishable body but is the tried-and-true knowledge obtained through cultivation.

People have considerable knowledge pertaining to the universe, life, science, philosophy, medicine, religion and the arts. All such knowledge is created by the source, which is the Mind. When we rediscover the supreme knowledge that the Mind is the source of life, we gain the ultimate understanding. Phenomena follow the Mind, and we are instantaneously liberated.

Enlightened buddhas, bodhisattvas and masters share common views on the nature of the Mind as it is; they share the same realization of the source of life, and accordingly they have the same understanding. In the acknowledgment of Creation and the source of all that is, there exists a singular perception of a universal power and, accordingly, the reverence to it. Enlightened Western religions also understand that their God—or the source of life—is no different from the God of another religion or civilization.

Everyone has a point of view, but often such views are opinions that are not in accordance with the truth. Having the right view is inseparable from understanding the nature of the Mind and the way phenomena are intimately connected to the source. The right view is concerned with what the Mind is, how to return to the Mind, and how the Mind functions and manifests all appearances. The right view is always centered on the Mind, just as the Bible is always centered on God. Any view that does not address the Mind may serve a temporary purpose but cannot truly guide people.

The right view and true practice focus on and implement how the Mind works and how it encompasses all existence. They focus on its intrinsic awakened nature as well as its emptiness and unborn-deathless nature. No one can live independently of the Universal Truth, the source of life that creates all appearances. Saints do not create the rules, but instead they recognize the source of life and live their lives in accordance with the nature and rule of that source.

No one can deviate from the most fundamental, ultimate source of life. Just as Buddhists cannot abandon the Mind, Western religions cannot stray from God. To do so would be considered heretical. Because human views tend to be narrowly focused and self-oriented, they are not views regarding the source of life. All practices should aim at the source of life in order for the practitioner to recover and affirm the true view of the Mind.

The attainment of a breakthrough in life requires a powerful desire and the strength to seek and return to the source of life. Otherwise, one will move from place to place like a homeless tramp. Even if you are blessed with wealth and power, life will be turbulent if you are oblivious to the existence of the source of life.

A life that is not rooted in recognition of the Mind is restless and unsettled. No matter how luxurious the resting place might be, it can only stay there temporarily. The innate nature of the Mind is emptiness, awareness and luminosity: This is the awakened-unborn nature. The Mind is its own master and is always at ease within its home. You, however, must realize this truth and live your life accordingly. Otherwise, you will be like a person who has a home to which he is reluctant to, or unable to, return.

A life lived without recognition of the original Mind but only with its various phenomena is like the short-lived morning dew and rootless spring grass. All efforts will produce only the fleeting scenery of seasonal change. However, if we can reflect inwardly to the source of thoughts to find and reveal the origin of all functions and the innate Mind, we can halt the endless cycle of life and death.

## Inwardly Resolving Our Life's Lessons

As human beings born into this world, we face various issues that are referred to as original sin in Western religions and negative karma in Buddhism. To put it simply, a person is born in order to complete certain lessons before he moves on to the next level. Without such lessons, we would not be here. In other words, the human journey in this world is not a beginning but the return to incomplete lessons.

The physical appearance of a human being, for example, simply cannot meet the standard of a heavenly being. Because our physical appearance is by no means comparable to the dignified Buddha and bodhisattvas, we should reflect upon our own thoughts and behavior. Because the way we function with our minds is not pure, we lack wisdom and focus. This insufficiency leads to the various flaws in our physical appearance. Think about it: Can an ill-tempered, narrow-minded person be pleasant-looking? Self-reflection here actually refers to the cultivation of our thoughts, not to sulking over our physical appearance.

Consequently, if one has a flawed appearance, physical ailments or lack of money, he or she must realize that such things are due to the failings in his or her life lessons. Because of those failings, we return to this world again and again. The purpose of the human journey in this world is to face our lessons and elevate the personal aspects that are incomplete and below the standard. Average people, having failed to understand this, bring past karma and incomplete lessons to this world. However, instead of trying to elevate themselves they simply accumulate more vexation and problems, thereby incurring another round of reincarnation.

We must cultivate ourselves in order to make real progress in life. We must identify our lessons, including anger, personality flaws, greed, over-eating, irritability, discrimination, jealousy, physical challenges, or whatever our own difficulties may be. We must realize that our imperfections are directly related to our thoughts. A different state of mind and thoughts will bring forth different physical conditions and personal relationships, thereby altering the environment in which we live.

All appearances are creations of the Mind. Therefore, we should approach all life lessons from the source—the Mind—instead of seeking answers outwardly. Buddhism is studied not only for the purpose of attaining enlightenment and nirvana, but Buddhism is also intended to address life lessons that, if left incomplete, will hinder the manifestation of our awakened nature and nirvana.

A person with a personality twisted by jealousy, alienation and judgmental thinking must learn to change from within. With such a polluted mind, even if the person prays and chants like Buddha he will be no more capable of helping him than dirt and dust would be. What is within the Mind is the mold that shapes its manifestations. Can a mind filled with attachment resonate with the Buddha? No, it is impossible.

The energy of the functions, emotions and feelings created by the Mind corresponds to the realms that resonate with that energy. If your thoughts are not on the same channel as the Buddha, you will not be able to resonate with Buddha. In such a case, the Buddha to which one shows devotion is no more helpful in life than a piece of copper, wood or stone. It is simply blind idolatry.

If my mind generates even one harmful thought, in that instant I am no longer a member of the monastic community because that thought is no longer in accordance with the monastic vows. Shaving or wearing a cassock does not make anyone a monk; it is only an outward appearance. The direct working of the Mind is its own true reflection, and therefore we must be responsible for our thoughts.

Does participation in a refuge ceremony qualify you as a true Buddhist? Perhaps it does in the moment because at that time your thoughts are proper, pure and oriented toward compassion and wisdom. However, if afterward you start to generate thoughts of conflict and attachment, in that moment you are no longer a disciple of the Buddha but are paying homage to a demon.

Does meditation dissipate disturbing thoughts? Not necessarily. The failure to eradicate attachment and troubled thoughts from within, the failure to identify the source of one's life and the failure to be responsible for one's thoughts can be compared to wiping a table with a dirty rag. The more we wipe, the more greed, anger, doubt, pride and inappropriate thoughts there will be. This can be compared to an attempt to keep the grass from growing by piling rocks on top of it. Even though there is a surface appearance of spiritual dedication and effort, the darkness within the mind proliferates like the wild grass, spreading season after season.

Unless you have the goal of eliminating your inner attachments, blind engagement in prayer, meditation or chanting practices is no better than seeking phenomena outwardly. You will not address the problems that have been brought into this life. Some people make little spiritual progress despite years of practice because, having temporarily set aside the dirty rags in their minds through the practice of meditation, they resume their old ways of talking and acting. Outside the meditation hall, they fill their minds with troublesome, disturbing thoughts.

Each individual brings countless issues to this life, and those issues require immediate attention in order to be resolved. If we replace real effort with empty talk on bodhi, nirvana and the nature of emptiness, we are much like a struggling primary school student who boasts about becoming a candidate for a master's degree or even a doctorate. What real progress can anyone make by praying, chanting and meditating with such a polluted mindset?

Unresolved life lessons are caused by the failure to identify our real problems. Ill-spent efforts are impractical and give only false hope. If the mind is filled with erroneous thinking, jealousy, alienation and judgmental opinions, religious chanting will be little more than lip service: It cannot prevent the twisting of the personality. Cultivation that is based on vexation and attachment will only deepen the negativity.

Some Buddhists appear to possess the right view to a certain degree. They are somewhat diligent, but no real progress can be shown. Their lack of progress proves that their understanding is ultimately not correct and their practice is misguided. If your practice cannot resolve real life lessons, your cultivation is not genuine.

If your learning and practice are not directly connected to your real issues, such continuous practice will inevitably produce an unhealthy disposition because there is no actual transformation in the level of your personality. It is a sign of misguided effort to behave one way inside the Zen hall but act another way outside. If your practice and day-to-day behavior are not mutually consistent, how can there not be a split in your personality?

A twisted personality is a reflection of an unhealthy mental state. Improper, deceiving speech reflects improper thoughts, which in turn nurture and strengthen the mind functions that resonate with negative realms and states of existence. We must observe our minds and practice consistency inside and outside the Zen hall. In the Zen hall, we should recognize the Mind's nature as egoless; it is of emptiness. Outside the Zen hall, we should maintain that same recognition of the Mind's egoless nature of emptiness.

The human mind has the same capability and potential that the Buddha mind has. The difference is that human beings do not know how to use the mind properly. They inadvertently create suffering, but the Buddha knows how to use the mind to create merit. The right understanding of reality is based on the concept that the Mind creates all dharma. The Mind, as the source of life, should be what each of us pursues.

Born into this life with baggage from a previous existence, we must identify our problems through self-reflection and strive to resolve them through inner work. Similarly, a student must first complete primary school before moving on toward higher education. Most people's present thoughts, speech and actions are far from their desired spiritual goals. Unaware of this reality, they develop the illusion of somehow reaching the Pure Land without clearing their attachments.

We must be responsible to ourselves in order to practice Buddhism. The workings of the source of life immediately manifest as the cause and result of this moment. The instant you take refuge in the Triple Jewels of Buddhism, your aspiration and compassion make you the person who takes refuge. However, if at this moment you generate vexation, you will instead become the vexation. You are responsible for resolving the issues you bring into this world. You must clean those dirty rags with pure thoughts. Otherwise, you are wiping a table with a dirty rag, which worsens the accumulation of defilement and makes it even harder to clean.

Unless you understand the nature of the Mind and focus on inner transformation, the more devoted you are to superficial practices, the more distorted your personality will become. Some Buddhists suffer from even more attachments than non-believers, because their minds have become confined within a strict pattern. You must practice inner reflection—seeing the darkness and learning to eliminate it from within—and strive to bring forth a mind of light, awareness, emptiness and clarity. This is cultivation.

Ancestral masters taught in simple acts of
dining and dressing;

Chanting and mantra invite the temptation of the demons.

Blinded by Buddhist scriptures in the thatch-roofed cottage;

One fails to recognize the voice of the true teaching hidden in

this dusty world.

# 2 THE UNIVERSAL TRUTH ALONE IS THE HOME OF ALL CONCEPTS

Early summer light floats and radiates;
Lazy south breeze slows down time.
Overnight all flowers blossom;
The next morning fallen petals are to be swept away.

## The Origin of Genesis

An understanding of reality can be compared to a map. It is critical that we select the path based on the right understanding in order to bypass the pitfalls and safely reach our destination. The pivotal points in self-transformation are the establishment of right understanding and the corresponding diligent practice. It is relatively simple to achieve the goal, if our actions match our understanding.

The purposes of spiritual cultivation are to unlock the wisdom and merit of the original Mind; to realize its unborn-deathless awakened nature for the benefit of ourselves and others; and ultimately to complete and perfect life in the path of the Buddha. Once the goal is clarified, we can discuss the kind of understanding that is necessary to reach the goal. Finally, we must choose a method and honestly engage in its practice.

Buddhism's core teachings of right understanding include the nature of the Mind, dependent origination, phenomena and principle, causality and impermanence: the fundamental principles of life and the universe. If a person claims to follow Theravada, Mahayana or Pure Land, he fails to capture the essence of the teaching. These schools are all methods or means that can be utilized for training in order to reach the goal. Ultimately, what matters is the path to the goal, not the sect a person follows.

Someone once asked me, during a group lecture, "If good deeds deliver one to heaven and bad deeds send one to the human realm or worse, how can this kind of back-and-forth reincarnation come to an end?" My answer was that we must return to the place from which we came. If you cannot return to the source of life, you can only have reincarnation. If you come from God and then return, reincarnation is ended. For those who believe the root is the Mind, returning to the Mind is the end of reincarnation. This is the most direct way to look at the question.

The main point of Zen practice is to find and abide in the source of life. The Buddhist term "reaching Buddhahood" simply means returning to the source of life and manifesting our original nature. All appearances are generated by the Mind; therefore, if anyone can return to the Mind, he or she will become the Buddha. The Mind is God. Regardless of religion, we must return to the Creator, or we will remain lost and suffer reincarnation.

Cultivation is aimed at calming the mind so that the creator within has control over its creation. A person who is lost and confused is unaware how the manifestation of God within works its wonders. That person therefore engages in creation under ignorance. If the Mind, or God, has no mastery over its creation, it will become attached to its own creations, grasping one creation after another like a monkey jumping from one vine to another, from past life to present life and continuing toward future life. Unless we return to the source and stop wandering among the creations of the Mind, our path between heaven and the human realm will be the cycle of reincarnation.

We must identify and live in harmony with the Creator in order to end reincarnation. If we fail to understand this fundamental principle, we will be trapped by various dogmas and theories and become limited by attachment to our particular religion. We must be clear about our chosen path's fundamentals and means: Does our practice move toward the purification of inner vexation and finding the Mind, or does it become mired in the illusionary concepts of life, death and enlightenment?

The universe has a source, from which natural disasters, human suffering and pain arise. Consequently, the saints and sages of ancient times searched diligently for the causes of such pain and problems, striving to resolve them through the implementation of religion. The ultimate purpose of every religion is to resolve the question of life and death. Every religion talks about the source of life, because it is the underlying context of religion.

Buddhism is no different in this respect. If we are clear about this point, we will not miss the original intent of Buddhism but will instead find the proper tools to fulfill its true purpose. Meditation, for instance, is for the purpose of bringing forth mental clarity and for learning how not to be swayed by habitual tendencies and sensory simulations. A mind that is clouded will constantly generate thoughts without awareness. Such a mind can only produce a life filled with pain and confusion.

Ignorance of the fact that life is the creation of the Mind is as if God were blindfolded, unable to see the floods, mountains, attachments and vexations that God has created. When we do not realize the original Mind, it is like a blind creator deceived by its own creations. An unclear mind is an ignorant mind: Because we do not know what we are creating, we cannot resolve what we have created. If God does not know who he has created, God's creations must wander in homelessness, unable to return home.

Eventually we realize, with the eradication of ignorance and attachment and the revelation of the true nature of the Mind, that all is self-created and therefore must be self-resolved. Thus we begin the process of dissolving, transforming and uplifting our lives. Buddhist teaching emphasizes awakening because it is a path of awakening, not a path of blind faith. We must open the Mind, let it shine through and wake to its creation.

It is futile to search for a better environment among the appearances created by the Mind. Heaven can be considered a better place to be, but it is still part of the reincarnation cycle and is therefore subject to change. Consequently, heaven cannot be the ultimate solution. Everything has a surface appearance and an underlying principle, so we must have a clear understanding before engaging in cultivation. Before we engage in any spiritual practice, we must understand its foundational theory and identify a consistent method based on that theory. When we understand those two things, we have a chance of success.

## Seek from the Mind, Not the Buddha

Buddhist teachings advocate a return to the source of life as the way to end the cycle of life and death. As Tao Yuanming's poem put it, "This life of mine is rootless; like dust in the field, it floats around with the wind, never in control of itself." A life based on changing appearances is like a rootless tree. Most people blindly depend on mind-made phenomena and grasp the thought of this moment as the "I." This is an attachment to existence in phenomena, so it is ignorance. Attachment and ignorance inevitably lead to a life of reincarnation, birth and destruction.

The Mind is formless, but it is also lively and energetic. It is able to create appearances continuously. In fact, the Mind is stable because it is formless. Despite the fact that with each moment of thought the physical body and the environment may change, they are all created by the same Mind. However, most people are ignorant of the Mind. Blind to its nature, they are unable to master it. They only know how to live in phenomena, which is like believing in God but trying to live apart from God. This is the irony of our life's expression.

The enlightened can see and experience the Mind clearly. The life of the unenlightened person follows narrow, twisting roads defined by misguided ideas. Such a path may be scenic, but it is always challenging to walk. If we constantly chase after that which changes in life and only live within the limited energy available there, we will have a rootless existence without any hope that we will ever find the unchanging source of life.

Master Zhi Xuan—also known as National Teacher Wuda—

was, by the age of five, an astute poet. Because his grandfather and father had not passed the imperial civil exam and therefore failed to become imperial scholars, they were determined that he would become one. Even as a child, Master Wuda was highly intuitive and wise. One day, his grandfather took him out for a trip. At the sight of a blossoming tree, the grandfather asked him to compose a poem. Without the slightest hesitation, he started: "With flowers blossoming, a tree is covered with red; when the blossoms pass, the tree is left with barren branches. One lonely blossom remains; but one more day the wind is destined to carry it away." Hearing the poem, the grandfather was moved to tears, realizing that his grandson would become a monk instead of fulfilling the family dream of imperial scholarship.

A human being, like a blooming tree, can achieve great accomplishments through consistent effort and hard work. However, these accomplishments are not life's destination but its process. As the poem says, "When the blossoms pass, the tree is left with barren branches." We always try to control impermanence with impermanence or to manage attachments with attachments. Our unrealistic hopes prevent the attainment of true understanding. While knowing that flowers pass after blooming, we cling to a hope in that "one lonely blossom." Unfortunately, it is just a matter of a breath or two before "the wind carries it away."

Thoughts come and go, so how can we control one thought with another? The body is impermanent, so how can one body try to control another? Life is impermanent unless we find the source: the Creator. Everything else is unstable and prone to change. Without guidance from the source of life, we tend to forget that we are ultimately responsible for our own creation. Those who live their lives in a happy-go-lucky fashion often engage in chaotic behavior, failing to understand life from a broader perspective.

Karma, as an accumulation of habits, is the driving force behind each thought. For each lifetime we spend in a particular realm, we accumulate one lifetime's worth of the habitual tendencies of that realm. Having been through countless reincarnations, we have accumulated countless habitual forces of karma, such as those of animals, demons or humans. Powerful beyond common imagination, the force of karma constantly pulls us in directions other than the one in which we should go.

People often think, "I know," or "I can." Without finding the root or source of life, the thoughts "I know" and "I can" are as fickle as duckweeds because they are subject to change. Today, you may believe you know and you can, but tomorrow the situation may be different. The only way for us to master life is to find and rest at the source of life, purify our delusion and become one with the Creator.

National Teacher Wuda once tried to advise the Tang Emperor Wuzong, who had issued orders for the destruction of Buddhism. Because the emperor sought immortality, Master Wuda composed a poem for him. "Heavenly being has the karma to dwell in heaven; not everyone who pursues immortality obtains it. The heavenly stork flies with its wings tilted, and the dragon's back can be slippery; no emperor ever lived past a century." Therefore, to be born into heaven one's mind must generate the corresponding functions. In other words, we must make the necessary effort. Desire alone will not suffice. It is one thing to desire something, but it is another thing to obtain it. They are two different realities.

Many Buddhists declare that because human life is impermanent and full of suffering they would not return to the human realm in the next life. However, is it really up to you to decide not to return? If you can first manage not to generate a single negative thought, you might be a bit closer to fulfilling your hope not to return to the human realm. Your desire to be a human and your manifestation as a human are two different things. Only when a clear, calm mind can take charge of each thought and make it pure and peaceful can anyone determine his own fate.

The Pure Land exists through a pure mind. An impure mind cannot generate clean energy despite its strong desire to do so. It is not a matter of desire. On a simpler level, if you hope for a pay raise, does it do any good just to plead with your boss if you are less than competent? You may worship Sakyamuni and Amitabha, but did they create you? Our creator is the Mind, where we seek our answers. Buddhas, bodhisattvas and their teachings do not do our spiritual work, they simply provide the guidance that supports it.

Effort brings results. It is not dependent on mercy from buddhas or bodhisattvas, who are just teachers who pass their knowledge on to you. If you do not apply yourself and consequently fail in your exams, what difference does it make to beg the teachers to let you graduate? You may plead with the teachers to teach you well, but ultimately what matters is the effort you make.

The elevation of life requires that you strive to make a

breakthrough in eradicating the blockage of attachments that blind you, so that the Mind—the Creator—can awaken. All the problems people face in life are the blind creations of the Mind. Most people either have no concept of the Mind or, even though they have learned of it through Buddhist scriptures and teachings, they are still unable to find it. Life without the understanding of the mind is a lost boat in the vast ocean, challenging one storm after another. It does not know the direction in which land will be found, so the only fate available is to sink into the abyss.

The goal of cultivation is to find the awakened nature and nirvana, which show a path toward a life of freedom, happiness and fulfillment. The key to the actualization of Buddhahood is to find the pure Mind. All predicaments and obstacles are created by the Mind, and therefore we should not blame the people or circumstances in our lives. We can only blame our own misuse of the Mind. Things are the way they are because we have committed such karma. As the saying goes, "What goes around comes around."

We cannot depend solely on a deity or Buddha for spiritual cultivation, a concept reflected in the saying, "God helps those who help themselves." In Buddhism it is said, "There are thirty-three levels of heaven, beyond which live the great immortals. The immortals themselves were initially humans, other than those who lacked resolution." The Mind is the source of all circumstances, whether favorable or difficult, and therefore we must turn to the Mind for all solutions. Life change does not begin with the manipulation of appearances. Can we simply turn a bad thought that has already appeared into a good one? We cannot. We can only stop generating bad thoughts altogether and generate good ones instead. ⍭

## Sacrifice Loved Ones or One's Mentor

The virtues of Buddha can serve as goals for our cultivation. The Buddha mind is free of obstacles, so it possesses great merits. Contrastingly, the mind of the ordinary person is narrow and therefore unable to create very much merit. The Buddha mind is aware and alert; therefore, it has wisdom. The common mind is not aware and alert; therefore, it has little wisdom. The Buddha mind is awake and pure; therefore, it is filled with wisdom and light. The ordinary mind is polluted and lacks awareness; thus there is little light and wisdom. The Buddha mind has the aspiration to liberate all living beings from suffering; the common mind is solely concerned with our personal welfare. The Buddha is full of compassion for all; human love is very conditional. The Buddha mind is free of ego; the human mind is inundated with attachments.

Even though it is true that the Mind is the Buddha, our mind has been polluted and become a befuddled Buddha. The countless negative tendencies latent in our small minds manifest a polluted environment. Such minds function without awareness. They are ignorant and occupied with ceaseless grasping.

⍭The highest compassion is the pure Mind, which encompasses all that is pure or impure, beautiful or ugly. It is constantly aware of the inseparability of its thoughts and actions from the essence, and it manifests the pure function of the Mind. The pure Mind is boundless. The selfless, pure Mind manifests the One Composite—

the Collective—which encompasses all phenomena in completeness. Every single thought is clear and consciously mastered, and every being is liberated. This is the state of Buddhahood.

Most people are unaware of their thoughts, which subconsciously divide the collective manifestation of the Mind into that which is desired, not desired, right, wrong, favored or hated. Such polluted thinking becomes complex and obscures our original nature. Though we ceaselessly generate thoughts, few of them are under our conscious control. A heavy burden of attachments and prejudice will cause a mind to lose awareness. The mind seems to be clearer regarding what it becomes attached to, but it automatically ignores everything else and this lack of awareness prevents us from true liberation.

Every manifestation results from the confluence of countless karmic conditions, but we can only perceive those on the surface. We do not know where a thought comes from, nor do we know where it goes. We do not know the reason a certain thought arises, nor do we know its karmic consequence. Because our minds lack wisdom, the burden of attachment limits our ability to see the various aspects, principles and appearances of a situation. We are burdened with vexations we cannot understand.

A pure mind is limitless. However, it lives in the current moment, and therefore every moment is infinite. For a pure mind, there is no past, present or future. A pure mind is like a mirror in which there is an appearance: There is an image, but when the appearance is gone the image is too. Our minds are initially pure, but gradually they become polluted by our self-created attachment till they are clouded with ignorance.

Attachments disappear when we replace our ego with the nirvana state of having a clear, self-contained mind. To reach nirvana, or to gain compassion and wisdom, we must rely on the pure mind.

Some people say that Buddhist practice requires the practitioner to be thoughtless. The term "thoughtless," however, does not mean anyone should eliminate the thought-generating function of his or her mind. Instead, it means the Mind should generate thoughts without being dependent on ego. Buddhist practice is intended to eradicate all obstacles and thereby reveal the innate Buddha nature of the Mind. Consider, for example, the talented person who is handicapped by poor judgment and prejudice. The solution is to help him get rid of his prejudice and allow him to show his talents.

A common mind is tainted by jealousy, alienation and judgmental thinking. With such a mind, everything a person encounters in life reflects these negative traits. The only way to get away from unpleasant people in life is to let go of negative thoughts in the mind.

Unless the root cause of the karmic appearances in your life is resolved in your mind, they will remain, because the habitual functioning of your mind acts like a hook to pull these appearances together. Therefore, in order to bring forth a real change in life, you must gradually let go of all the greed, anger and confusion in your mind.

A story from Buddhist scripture tells of a group of relatives who traveled to the south on business. They brought a guide, who was not a relative. One day, they arrived at a temple in a vast field. The local custom required them to sacrifice a fellow traveler so as to travel safely through the field. The group finally came to an agreement that the guide should be sacrificed, because he was the only one who was not a relative. Accordingly, the sacrifice was carried out. Thus the group, without a guide, got hopelessly lost in the field and everyone died.

Correct knowledge is like the guide in this story. Neglecting the correct knowledge in preference to familiar thoughts, even when one's mind is filled with irritation and trouble, is the sacrifice of the guide. Such is the case with many self-described Buddhists.

Views that are incorrect and misguided attach to a person's mind like skin attaches to flesh. To separate them, one must go through a painful process, as illustrated in Master Huangbo's poem: "It is no easy feat to separate from earthly matters; many hold onto the last straw, unable to let go. Afraid of facing bone-penetrating cold, how could one capture the immense fragrance of the winter plum blossoms?"

Buddhist practice is impossible without the guidance of correct knowledge. We need it to solve the problems and issues in life. So, should we sacrifice correct knowledge for the more familiar thoughts of negativity? How can real progress be made if one continues to associate with these "relatives"?

Another Buddhist story tells of a father and a son: One night the father asked the son to go to the village on business the next day. So, the son got up early and went to the village. Not knowing what business his father had in mind, the son wandered around in the village the entire day, getting rejected everywhere he went. At night he came home, starved and exhausted. The father asked, "What business did you go to the village for without asking me first?"

Buddhist practice is not blind meditation and self-deprecation. The goal is to purify our minds so superficial effort will not achieve it. It is certainly hard work to chant and meditate, but is your goal to purify the mind or to run yourself down? The essential difference is whether we channel our hard work toward the purification of the mind. Otherwise, all our efforts will be in vain, like the son who wasted a whole day in the village.

We tend to define and label every person and incident with prejudicial attachments. A lay practitioner once asked me how to keep from labeling things. I replied that every thought is a label. Do you know your own thoughts? How do you avoid labeling things if you do not know your own thoughts? Thoughts are like hidden thieves: One has to find the thieves before he can catch any. So, one must calm the mind and stabilize it in order to achieve his goals.

Those who practice in order to achieve goals follow one school, one sect and one master. They follow the guide's instruction and practice at a slow but steady pace until they reach their destination. At that point, their guide disappears and in his place is a calm, clear mind. If one fully understands the goal and methods, he will not be confused by the question of cause and effect.

Continually remind yourself to work from the root of the cause. Examine old habits and attachments through introspection, and gradually let go of them. This process is even more effective than years of meditation. When striving to recover a calm, clear mind, you will run into difficulties and setbacks in the form of "loved ones and relatives." They could be familiar thoughts of attachments and judgment, but you must let them go before you can reach your destination.

If you do not practice introspection so as to eliminate old habits and attachments but instead allow them to remain, any attempt to meditate or practice chanting will create inner conflict. It is like trying to take over a mountaintop by dividing your troops and sending them in various directions. It only makes the task more difficult.

The pure, empty nature of the Mind can dissolve all attachments and troubles. All issues and problems cease to exist when we possess wisdom, compassion and merit. As Master Hanshan put it, "The deep-blue ocean is vast and empty; a singular moon shines in the dark, cold, night sky; miles and miles of clouds clear off right in front of my eyes; the self-awakened Mind of stillness becomes one with the crystal-clear moon." So, too, we realize the Pure Mind, which is peaceful and selfless; a void, like a vast, clear ocean without any waves or disturbances.

The more we practice, the calmer we will be. Having set aside vexation, attachment and delusion, we experience a deepening of concentration, wisdom and merit. Ultimately, the intrinsic awakened, clear, empty nature of the Mind emerges like the moon on a dark, cold night. Upon enlightenment, all thoughts clear away to reveal miles and miles of cloudless sky, where only the intrinsic awakened nature is present, shining like a crystal-clear moon. With wisdom, compassion and light, the path to Buddhahood begins. This is not simply about accumulating worldly prosperity or heavenly rewards. It is not attainable through ritualistic practices but only through the continuous eradication of all greed, hatred and delusion within the mind.

## All Rivers Flow East

The clear, calm mind, being free of attachments, troubles and accumulated habits, is the true Buddha. Before meals, Buddhists must pay respect and tribute to the Three Jewels: The Buddha, the Dharma and the Sangha." Master Zhaozhou once said, "The metal Buddha cannot survive the melting pot, the wooden Buddha cannot survive fire, and the mud Buddha cannot survive water; but the true Buddha comes from within." The true Buddha is the Mind and the true Buddha is formless, so how can anyone pay tribute to the Buddha? The sutra states: "The best tribute to Buddha is through diligent effort." To pay tribute to the Buddha is to manifest the pure Mind; it is to generate the pure Mind and pure action that lead to pure merit.

Similarly, the placement of scriptures at the altar is not a true sign of respect for the dharma, because the dharma is more than scripture alone. The scriptures only describe the nature and principles of the Mind; the true dharma is the dharma of the Mind. Everything encompassed by the Mind is the dharma. The pure Mind is emptiness; it is egoless, tranquil, unborn and deathless. It is perfect, encompassing the Hua-yen Realm, Fa-hua Realm, Surrangama Realm and the various realms that arise from Samadhi. The Mind is the source of life, and by its nature it encompasses all realms, which mutually penetrate and merge. To pay respect to the dharma is to reveal and abide in the nature and function of the Mind.

The payment of respect to the Sangha starts by generating the right thoughts from the pure Mind. The common understanding of "right thought," however, is merely a convenient concept based on duality. In other words, it is a kind of positive thinking based on mental discrimination. In fact, right thoughts only arise through the eradication of ego attachment. Only thoughts that arise from an egoless mind can be pure and free from life and death. Otherwise, there remains a duality that is conditional, defiled, contaminated, deluded and troubled. It is not right thought to have positive thoughts that arise as a result of particular people, times and places. Right thought is the pure function that arises from the truth that is universal; from the truth that transcends time and space.

Only by understanding the truth can we escape the predicament of irritations and illusions and recover the Mind, which is peaceful, calm, clear and self-mastered. Consider the following story: Once a government official called Wang Changshi paid a visit to Master Linji. He asked the master whether the monks at his temple read scriptures and studied Zen. Master Linji said, "They do not." Wang Changshi, somewhat surprised, then asked, "Well, what do they do?" Master Linji said, "I just ask them to become Buddha." Hearing this, Wang said, "Golden dust is valuable, but it causes pain if it falls into the eyes."

Scriptures are valuable, like gold, but if the dust falls into our eyes it can cause discomfort or even blind us. The Mind is originally pure, but too much specious scriptural ideology or egocentric thinking can blind the eyes of the Mind. Master Linji does not teach scriptures and doctrines; instead he goes straight to the source of thoughts and appearances in the present moment. On this source he begins his teaching.

Spiritual ideas taught for convenience are designed to inspire faith and practice so that people might begin on the path. It is like taking several connecting buses to get to the final destination. Eventually you will reach the final stop, but the route is not a direct one. The ancient saying, "All rivers flow east," means that each river has its own course but eventually flows into the ocean. The Mind is the ocean of self-nature; the ocean of merit. Accordingly, whether in Zen, Pure Land, Mahayana or Hinayana, all must go back to the Mind.

Everyone has innate Buddha nature. This concept is universally true among all sects of Buddhism. This innate Buddha nature, like the Mind, is the foundation for liberation. However, it is not enough to study liberation. Instead, we must know why it happens, how it happens and what happens afterward. Unless we truly understand these questions, our efforts will have only half their intended effect.

If the principles a sect advocates are directly related to the Mind, Buddha nature, dependent origination and karma, those principles are in accordance with the truth. This sect is worth learning about and practicing, because it has the ability to lead a person from its convenient teachings to the ultimate goal of liberation. The benefit of our practice and ultimately the issue of life and death are determined by the key factor of the sect's principles.

Different diseases require different medicines, but all diseases are signs of imbalance among the Four Elements of the body. These imbalances originate in an unhealthy mind. Therefore, erroneous views and behaviors comprise the real cause of disease. Whether it is a disease in the worldly sense or in the spiritual sense, we must start from the Mind in order to cure that disease. This is why the teachings of every sect must center on the Mind.

It is good to read scriptures, but we must remember that the scriptures describe the transcendence of this world; the imperturbable self-nature of the Mind and the presence of this self-nature, or the pure Mind. The existence of the essence of the pure Mind as a "thing-in-itself" is the Great Samadhi of Surrangama, which is the main concept conveyed by the Surrangama Sutra. However, if we study the scripture with old habits and attachments, the ideas we pick up cannot help us manifest the pure self-nature that is the Surrangama Samadhi. Studying the scriptures in such a dualistic fashion only creates more confusion and doubt, ultimately hindering the quest for liberation.

Does Amitabha Buddha come forth to deliver us when we leave this world? This is not exactly so. The real issue is whether one's mind can manifest the realm of Amitabha. Otherwise, no matter how many people help us in the ceremony we cannot reach Paradise, so Amitabha Buddha will not come to deliver us. It is essential to understand this if we want to practice the Pure Land method, or we will become confused and delay the establishment of true practice. We must first clarify the basic principles before plunging into full practice. Otherwise, how can we reach our destination using an unclear map? If one practices by following a speculative mind filled with attachments, there is no choice but to manifest a realm filled with attachments.

A wealthy man of an ancient time collected pearls. Another wealthy man followed suit. However, the pearls he bought were not real pearls but only made of fish eyes. Later, both men fell ill. A doctor told them that medicine made of ground pearl powder would cure them. The one with the real pearls did as instructed and became well. The one with the fake pearls did not believe it when the doctor claimed his pearls were not genuine. The doctor proved it by soaking them in water. Without medicine made with real pearls, the second man died.

Similarly, people have so much confidence in their understanding and practice—including mystical or miraculous experiences—that they are certain nothing can go wrong. However, if our practice and efforts fail to find and abide in the Mind, they are no better than fake pearls. At the critical moment of life and death, they will be worthless.

We suddenly wonder, when faced with predicaments, whether our usual efforts will be enough to save us. However, the principle that can save one's life is beyond the distinction of good or evil. Only the principle that all is manifested by the Mind can rescue us from the predicaments and issues of life. If you cannot even identify the principle of enlightenment and be clear on that, please do not talk about enlightenment. In such a case, no refuge can be found and life will be difficult indeed.

Every sect claims that its teachings are supreme, but the true practice is that of understanding the Universal Truth and having the means to apply, experience, understand and manifest its principles. Strictly speaking, most people, instead of studying true Buddhism, merely walk in circles outside the door. They seek the path of convenience. Real Buddhist practitioners recognize that all phenomena are inseparable from the Mind. They realize the Mind, take responsibility for it, and function differently with the Mind in order to effect change and create the future. This is a true practice that brings real benefit.

An understanding of liberation and truth is universal to the teachings of the enlightened beings. These are the teachings we must learn; the rest are merely for the sake of convenience. For example, Buddhist practice requires that we take refuge and understand the Five Precepts. Some sects require a vegetarian diet, some the taking-up of practices and vows, and so forth. These requirements have been devised in order to support our spiritual cultivation. They are like individual vehicles that take people from one place to another. They do not necessarily deliver us to the final destination. Instead, their significance is to help people gradually let go of accumulated habits and attachments.

Even if we were to practice the Bodhisattva precept for a hundred years, without enlightenment we would not escape the cycle of life and death. Even after achieving enlightenment, if we cease to practice the cycle will resume. If our test score is just 0.0001 below the level required for admission, we will not be admitted to the university. Similarly, if we are just a step away from enlightenment we must still practice. There is no room for compromise. Spiritual work is very practical; there are no accommodations for vague notions. We must ask ourselves whether our understanding and practice can save us from the vexations and troubles in life. If the answer is no, we must again start the process of self-reflection.

We must eliminate old attachments and habits and reveal a soft, pure, egoless mind before we can bring about change and elevate our course through life. Only after dismantling our erroneous mentality, fully understanding the truth that all is created by the Mind and living accordingly can we find a refuge in life. Otherwise, our lives will remain in disarray.

A hundred people have a hundred ways of thinking, and this demonstrates the proliferation of individuality. However, each and every person can generate his or her own thoughts. The understanding of the nature of the Mind is not about each individual's unique thinking but is about each person's innate ability to generate unique thoughts. Other than the Universal Truth, no earthly knowledge can solve all of life's issues.

Buddha and Bodhisattva are appearances, as is heavenly light. Appearances are generated from the Mind. Kind people and mean people, beautiful landscapes and filthy landfills are all creations of the Mind. Therefore, appearances are not our true refuge because phenomena are dependent on the underlying essence. The essence beyond the appearance of a Buddha or a pile of feces is the same. Like everything else, they are created by the Mind.

Your relatives, friends and colleagues, as well as your problems and vexations, are all here to encounter. Because the mental state and thinking in your mind connects to the situation they represent, your mind resonates with their frequencies. When your mind is filled with kindness, compassion and pure thoughts, Buddha appears to you. Different functions of the Mind lead to different appearances, but the principle governing the Mind's function remains the same.

The disconnection of daily life from spiritual practice finds us failing to manage our lives, even though ultimately we hope to achieve a wholesome life and enlightenment. Unless we attain the pure, clear aspect of the Mind, what kinds of situations can we expect to have in our lives? There is a direct correlation between the function of the Mind and what manifests in our lives. Every second of every person's life is governed by this principle. It does not apply only in the final moment of life when we may either ascend to heaven or descend into hell.

The point of spiritual cultivation is to implement the universal principle of the Mind. The scriptures all follow this basic principle, just as all laws and regulations must abide by a national constitution. Any scripture that deviates from the principle of the Mind is either illegitimate or misinterpreted by practitioners. Therefore, all spiritual cultivation must gravitate toward, recognize and merge with this principle of the Mind.

> I enter this life already wearing an opera costume;
> For better or for worse, I play my role well.
> Barely taking a moment of rest backstage,
> I hear the chimes and drums signaling
> the change to a new role.

# 3 BRING THE ENLIGHTENMENT OF ZEN SCRIPTURES INTO PRACTICE

A white egret flies out of autumn reeds across misty water;
A swallow returns to its dry nest from

a trip in the cold mountains.
A lonely moon shines brilliantly up in the sky;
Deep into the night I am sleepless.

## To Cultivate Spirituality Is to Find One's True Destination in Life

The understanding of Buddhist teaching means an understanding of the Mind—the source of life—as well as the relationship between ourselves and the world we have created. Inevitably, we encounter difficulties and pains in life, but the recognition of the cause of suffering is the beginning of the end of suffering. First, we see how appearances are created, then we change the structure through which appearances are created. Having redirected the energy of the source to a new structure, we create better appearances in life. In other words, one lives a better life.

Conventional knowledge is not based upon the Universal Truth. For example, scientific analysis is flawed by concepts of duality, such as the observer versus the observed, and therefore its conclusions are prone to change and relativism. However, if specific conditions were not imposed, scientific research might yield surprising outcomes. The imposition of limits on conditions and factors means the conclusions thus derived are hypothetical at best. Dualistic research is limited because it sets forth certain conditions as prerequisites.

Conventional knowledge, such as medicine, science and philosophy, results from duality so it can solve only certain human issues. It cannot correct the fundamental problem. For instance, medicine might ease your symptoms but it will not eliminate the root cause of your disease. Those who are health-minded pay attention to nutrition and tonics, but still they get sick. The lack of any particular tonic or medicine is not the cause of disease. Instead the root cause lies within the mind.

Buddhist teaching is about the nature of the Mind. However, people generally believe in seeking the truth outside the Mind. As a scripture put it, "Enlightenment may arise in an instant, eradicating all conventional concepts, but the specifics of phenomena can only be eliminated gradually and in stages." Therefore, considerable effort is needed in order to apply our understanding to real life. Understanding does not equate to actual accomplishment, however, because old habits or incomplete understanding prevent the effective application of the truth.

The truth is not necessarily internalized simply because a person hears it. Dissolving our deep-rooted opinions and biases requires time. Despite our acknowledgment that everyone has the original Mind and all appearances are created by the Mind, when faced with setbacks and challenges we find it difficult to accept and dissolve them.

If we can truly understand the following five stages for reaching Zen enlightenment, and if we adopt them as the guidelines for our constant contemplation, we can build a foundation for future enlightenment.

## The First Stage: Understanding the Principles Regarding the Nature of the Mind

Why can eyes see appearances? Why can ears hear sounds? Without the mind, our eyes and ears are lifeless. It is a function of the mind to bring forth the appearances, and our eyes and ears are simply channels through which the appearances are presented to us. We will not be able to see or hear unless the mind carries out the corresponding functions of seeing and hearing. As a further example, if your mind is lost in thought, even if there is an open book in front of your eyes you will not grasp the book's content because the mind is not attuned to the reading. A colloquial saying puts it this way: "A man does not shed tears easily, unless he is touched by the soft spot of his heart."

Most of us think in dualistic terms. We create self-centered mental structures that support judgmental thoughts. The purpose of enlightenment is to dismantle such a structure; to realize and directly recognize the Mind. This is what Zen calls "our own duty." The Mind is the source of life, from which all emotions, successes and failures originate. The function of the formless Mind can create, in the present moment, appearances as small as a thought and as vast as the universe.

The collective of myriad conditions and appearances manifested by the present-moment function of the Mind is the singular "I" of the moment. It is also the Collective, with which we resonate and live. Form follows the Mind like a shadow follows the body. The collective appearance of the moment, however, is the expression of the Mind itself. It is the result of the Mind and its corresponding functional structure in this very moment. Thus we have the saying, "Appearance is inseparable from emptiness." Appearances and emptiness are mutually supportive, interchangeably serving as the foreground and background. The encounters and appearances in each moment are the corresponding manifestations of the Mind's function. Collectively, they are the ever-changing, moment-to-moment expression and countenance of the formless Mind.

The Mind functions constantly, and as it does the body and environment—as well as their corresponding factors and conditions—are present, just as the shadow is created by the body under the sun. Therefore, whenever we perceive imperfection in others we should practice self-reflection; those imperfections simply resonate with the flawed personality in our own minds. Remember, similar energies flock together just as birds of a feather do. You are not distinct from those around you.

An unenlightened mind, like a dusty mirror that shows fuzzy reflections, contains incomplete or even distorted opinions. Most any person will mistake the distorted, fuzzy functions of the Mind as his or her "self." Like a spot of dust on the mirror, this "self" is not the true source of life but is just a momentary manifestation, subject to dissolution. We may think a certain way one moment, but with the very next moment our thinking can change. This "self," which is a function of the Mind, is ever-changing, rootless and impermanent.

People generally mistake the changing functions of the Mind as their self-identity, but it is illusory to do so. This identification with the functions of the Mind, which originate from the Source, causes further instability in the mind of the individual. The true self is the Mind, formless but omnipresent. It projects a constantly changing, momentary self through its functions. While dust brings about fuzziness, without the mirror as the foundation there would not be any fuzzy reflections. Consequently, it is because of this true Mind that defiled functions can arise, bringing forth illusions, irritations and attachments.

Our perception of "self" is actually part of the Mind's manifestation. The observer is also a part of the observed, as the observer and the observed appear simultaneously. However, in non-duality there is no so-called observer. Energy is indivisible, and its state of existence is a result of the present karmic conditions created by the Mind. In the fundamental understanding of the Mind, there are neither people nor appearances beyond the Mind.

According to Zen teaching, if you killed your parents you must repent to the Buddha; but if you were to kill the Buddha or a patriarch, where could you go to repent? In other words, when people generate harmful thoughts in response to a certain person or a situation, they should repent to Buddha; but whatever they commit is not actually against the Buddha. So, why should they repent to Buddha? The Mind is the source of every cause and effect. We must understand the emptiness of the causal mind and know that the resulting phenomena simultaneously function as the essence and the appearance.

Buddha is a sentient being free of worry. Contrastingly, a sentient being is a Buddha burdened by worries. When the pure Mind is revealed and we can abide with ease in its awakened nature without being moved by habitual tendencies, we can then dissolve our sufferings and attachments. This is the true repentance to the Buddha. However, when we repent with a worry-ridden mind before a Buddha statue, it is just a convenient practice. Unless we understand what repentance is really about, our actions before the statue are meaningless. Neither Buddha nor the bodhisattvas cause the emergence of negative thoughts. In order to dissolve negativities we should repent from the very source where these thoughts arise.

People generally cannot bring themselves to face their own problems and faults. Thus the Buddhist teachings use various convenient methods such as meditation and repentance to guide people gradually toward the root cause, which is one's own mind. If we focus solely on the surface appearance of repentance—acting with respect in the presence of the scriptures and temple but forgetting all about respect and self-reflection in daily life—it will be impossible to dissolve our inner faults and attachments.

Many people diligently worship Buddha. They may chant, meditate, repent and take spiritual vows, but they ignore their negative behaviors. This is like taking lots of vitamins that have no impact on the cause of illness and will therefore not produce a cure. Unable to face their mistakes, people constantly generate negative thoughts such as greed, anger, gluttony, jealousy and alienation. These thoughts are a poison that no vitamin in any amount can counteract. How can such a practice be in accordance with the principle of causality?

The worship of Buddha, chanting and meditation, and repentance are simply tools for use in the cultivation of spirituality. One does not guarantee that work will be completed just because he holds tools in his hands, because these tools are not the cause of suffering and reincarnation. The real lesson of life occurs when we have a mind that is out of control. Such a mind is filled with attachments and judgmental opinions that arise depending on people, circumstances, locations and objects. We must confront it and resolve a few key questions: When do I generate negative thoughts? In whose regard do I generate them? Why do I generate such thoughts? Where do negative thoughts come from?

Spiritual cultivation has only one certain path: the path by which we come to understand the nature of the Mind. Whatever thoughts arise from the Mind, there is a simultaneous energy response. This is the direct link between the cause and the result. When you becomes irritated in regard to a situation, the idea in your mind is definitely not about the truth of the Mind. Instead, it constitutes a self-centered mentality.

It is common to hear the complaint, "Why do I always run into this kind of problem? Why is it always me?" Actually, the reason is expressed in a saying: "Mountains and rivers move easily; habit and personality hardly change." Similar experiences will be repeated if our old habits are not corrected and resolved. The human mind attaches itself to certain traits of the appearances in this present moment, and it follows them in order to create the next moment of one's life. Therefore, it is not that you keep running into similar experiences but that you continually create attachments to similar karmic conditions. Thus the same results are generated again and again.

Predicaments and pain are the most demanding teachers in life. They come to our last line of defense with the warning that we should correct past behaviors and start a new life. Lacking awareness of our inner habitual tendencies and attachments, we allow them to generate repetitions of problems and predicaments. Unconsciously, we hypnotize ourselves until those habits and attachments are created, and in our self-righteousness we follow them.

## The Second Stage: Familiarize Yourself with the Nature of the Mind

Based on our understanding of the Mind, we must become familiar with its principles. In addition to knowing that vexations and attachments, the past, present and future, and all emotions are manifestations of the Mind, we must be aware of the situations and karmic conditions that resonate with the Mind's functions. Despite all the meditation, chanting, repenting and resolution, we will be lost if we do not eliminate old habits and attachments from the mind. Such a misguided religious practice is only a superstition; it will not bring real progress. After all, one cannot harvest oranges from an apple tree.

You should frequently read the scriptures and masters' recorded teachings, and you should ponder the principles of the Mind. When faced with any obstacle, ask yourself whether you still believe it is the fault of others or if you have created it. Your practice will not be steady and solid unless you apply, in daily life, the truth that "the Mind is the source of life." If we do not make efforts to familiarize ourselves with the principles of the Mind but instead allow erroneous concepts to guide our behavior, we will submit to the chronic poisoning of ourselves.

As an ancient saying put it, "Staying long in a fish market, one no longer smells the stench." What we habitually view as right or wrong is merely a habit but not a fact. Our habits blind us to the point that we can no longer tell right from wrong. Any principle that deviates from the nature of the Mind is ultimately speculation; any action not guided by the principles of the Mind is just a show. The continuous attachment to phenomena, born out of ignorance, creates a cyclical existence that can be compared to episode after episode of opera. We must remember that stage life is not real life. Master Hanshan once said, "No need to compete for entrance into the action; one scene after another the opera goes on and on. All of a sudden the chimes and drums stop; all the actors wonder where to return."

A person may acquire considerable knowledge and skill in life, but these attainments do not necessarily help solve the issues of life. A doctoral degree may not ensure a happy life or the ability to resolve all the problems a person has created for himself. It takes true wisdom to elevate our quality of life, and this of course requires the understanding of liberation and practice.

The purpose of cultivation is to guide us back to the Mind in order to utilize it and master our lives. If you master your mind, you will master your life. Most of the irritations people experience are related to specific persons or situations. Due to the lack of understanding, our inner habitual tendency and attachment collide with these persons and situations, in turn triggering even stronger habits and attachments. A mind that is out of control can create negative karma that will, over time, create adversities such as disease, poor relationships, a difficult environment, pollution and so forth. These are extensions of the flaws within the mind.

One must know the origin of a problem in order to resolve it. All issues in this world come about due to our deviation from the principle of the Mind. The Mind's nature is emptiness, whereas we constantly have this strong sense of "I:" "I feel," "I see" and "I think." This "I" has all kinds of "shoulds" and "musts." Many people seem to understand teaching on the Mind as long as they remain in the temple or the meditation hall, but once outside they drop it and again walk around with their sense of "I." We should remember that every suffering and attachment is due to our deviation from the emptiness of the Mind.

The direct path to enlightenment is to look directly into the Mind and inquire sincerely. When studying Zen, we should not distract ourselves with too much knowledge or writings that are not in accordance with the principles of the Mind. These things are of little help in our practice and should therefore be set aside. Most of us are already over-burdened with erroneous opinions that would take a lifetime to correct, so there is no need to add more. Some of them can actually create emotional disturbances and a false sense of elation and joy. It is ultimately meaningless to rely on these fleeting experiences because, in such circumstances, we will drift along with the impermanent flow of appearances and fail to master our lives.

True cultivation is as simple and straightforward as breathing. There is nothing fancy about it. The Mind is formless but alive and alert, and it encompasses all. The poet Su Dongpo described the Mind thus: "Within the void is hidden everything—the flowers, the moon and the pavilions." To really escape from the suffering of life and death, we must look within and peel off our old habits and attachments layer by layer. The path to nirvana begins with our mind. "All Buddhas achieve nirvana through the Mind; the Mind is clear and pure, free of defilement." When the mind is purified, the light of wisdom shines forth naturally.

### The Third Stage: Applying the Principle of the Mind

Given our understanding of the Mind and its principle, we must put it into the real context and apply it to daily life. Burdened with old habits and narrow-mindedness, we tend to become irritated when faced with difficulties. Therefore, the practice of self-reflection that establishes the individual's mind in the principle of the Mind is critically important. When faced with a setback, we must be alert to the fact that the difficulty indicates a certain fault in how we have applied our mind. We have strayed from the spaciousness and selflessness of the Mind and become entangled with dualistic, judgmental opinions. Therefore, we must apply the principle of the Mind and let go of such entanglements.

Our views are the foundation of our actions; consequently, incorrect views lead to improper actions and results. If we cannot apply the principle of the Mind to how we perceive life's situations, we are lost. Our understanding is not thorough and our mind does not possess a calm focus. In real life, we must test the principle in specific situations and be aware that the irritations and annoyances of people and things are actually created within our minds. Thus the way one uses his or her mind becomes the basis of our life's various appearances. We are responsible for our own fate, because the cause of every problem lies within.

Impure and disturbed, the average person's mind lacks good judgment. The so-called discernment of right versus wrong is actually a matter of personal taste and habit, reflecting the ego. Thus we have the saying, "The devil comes from the mind." To a certain degree, improper thoughts can be considered a kind of devil. Thought is energy. We unconsciously generate one bad thought after another, gradually accumulating a strong negative energy that builds up bad habits. As erroneous thinking accelerates like a snowball, growing to such an extent that it is beyond our control, we become unconscious with regard to our thinking and behavior. When you find yourself in a predicament, you should realize the situation indicates that your action has deviated from the principle of the Mind. When faced with such a predicament, you should immediately adjust. Return to the principle of the Mind.

## The Fourth Stage: Perceive the Principle Regarding the Nature of the Mind

A clear perception of the nature of the Mind prepares a person for enlightenment. After seeing the nature of the Mind, we must abide in it despite the continuous changes in our physical state or the environment, as if we are walking in emptiness. Then we will actually know that the Mind and the phenomena do not impinge upon each other. However, to state what it is like is to miss the point. Within the state of all-pervasive awakening, the physical body, environment and landscape change constantly. The true void of the Mind manifests all the causes and conditions that support this present moment, but the interior and exterior are as one. Only then can we truly accept the principle that all phenomena are inseparable from the Mind; that all is created and manifested by the Mind.

Can we ever expect to achieve enlightenment without truly understanding, becoming familiar with and practicing the principle of the Mind in our lives? How can we reach the east without finding it on the map, studying the route and landmarks, and progressing toward it? The question of whether we will achieve enlightenment solely depends on whether we focus on the nature of the Mind. Cultivation will not last unless it is focused on the principle of the Mind. Regardless of how long we meditate or how many scriptures we recite and memorize, we will eventually stop, forget and regress. There is no point in cultivating something that is created and ultimately destined for destruction. It is merely pretentious talk and acting; it is not the Buddha dharma.

Our karma is the creation of our own mind, so we must take responsibility. The Mind is the true cause; thoughts are its functions, and appearances are its outcome. Cultivation is based upon this principle. The Buddha dharma transcends the birth and death of phenomena. It is the "of Mind" nature. It is liberation, or the union of emptiness and transcendental existence; and the Mind is Buddha.

The Buddha dharma is the path of non-duality, in which thoughts and appearances are one, the body and environment are one, and emptiness and existence are one.

The realization of the nature of the Mind requires that we practice self-reflection on a daily basis in order to dissolve negative thoughts as they appear. Whether it is Zen inquiry or koan study, the purpose is to identify the origin of thoughts. If our mind is filled with the habitual negativity of vexation, judgmental opinions and attachments, it is obviously impossible to find the origin of thoughts. We must train according to the principle of the Mind in order to tame old habits and see the origin of thoughts. After identifying the origin of thoughts, we then break through it in order to reach the state of non-duality, which is enlightenment. All Buddhas and enlightened masters achieve the Dao through enlightenment.

Master Da'an, of the Tang Dynasty, was already well versed in the Tripitaka and Twelve Divisions of Mahayana scripture when he committed himself to spiritual life at Mt. Huangbo. His mind, however, was unsettled. He lacked an understanding of the nature of the Mind, Buddhahood, enlightenment and the full attainment of Dao. If we are committing time and effort to practice, we should make progress instead of being wishy-washy. Master Da'an, having the wisdom, merit and determination to achieve enlightenment, went on a pilgrimage to study with Master Baizhang. When Master Baizhang inquired as to the purpose of his visit, Master Da'an said, "I want to know what Buddha is." Master Baizhang replied, "You are looking for the bull while riding it."

Master Da'an, upon this reply, realized that cultivation is not seeking from without; instead, it is the inner dissolution of vexation and illusions, a dissolution that will reveal the original Mind. With such a revelation, you attain the ability to hear, see and demonstrate your Buddha nature. You are the only one who can generate your thoughts.

Master Da'an, having recognized the nature of the Mind, asked Master Baizhang, "Then what?" Master Baizhang replied, "Then you ride the bull home." So, upon enlightenment, having found "the bull," we can go home. We put an end to aimless wandering, as described in the Yuanjue scriptures, "the knowledge that illusions in the void put an end to samsara." If a person rubs his eyes, he will see illusory color and form in the air. Some might say the form exists outside, but others say it is created by the eyes. While it is a complete misunderstanding to say that vexation comes from outside, neither is it a correct understanding to view it as coming from inside.

Illusory forms come neither from outside nor from within. If vexation comes from outside, it has nothing to do with you. If the vexation is from within, you will never be free from it. Vexation is a kind of illusion, or the result of attachment. As soon as the eyes are settled again, one realizes that fundamentally the illusion was never really there. If we can dissolve our illusionary thinking and attachment and thereby reveal the original purity of the Mind, we will leave behind the cause of reincarnation.

## The Fifth Stage: Abide in the Nature of the Mind ... and Use the Mind

We must continually strive to abide in the nature of the Mind after we attain enlightenment, because old habits still threaten to replace the newly revealed Dao with vexation and judgmental opinions. When Dao and the realization of it are present, there is no vexation or conflict. The Mind is as pure as it was, and it is free of ego. We must manifest from the formless source of life, enlivening the Mind, dwelling in nothing. When function arises and ends instantaneously without the tendency to cling, it reflects the emptiness of the pure, egoless Mind. After enlightenment, we abide in the Dao. It is from here that we begin to put an end to birth and death, whereby we attain the basis for liberation.

Master Da'an then asked Master Baizhang how to maintain it. Master Baizhang replied, "Like a herder, one should take up a staff and ward the bull away from any farm field." When we can prevent the bull from eating grass or grain—or cultivate mastery over the mind and have total control over thoughts—we will have the ability to transform vexations.

Master Da'an had served as the head cook for Master Weishan. When he eventually replaced him as the abbot, he said in his ceremonial speech, "I lived in Mt. Weishan for thirty years. I ate the Weishan food, I even passed Weishan dung, but I never learned any Weishan Zen. All I did was watch over a water buffalo." His water buffalo was the Mind: When the Mind is tempted by vexation, illusion and other negative thoughts, the buffalo is eating grass stealthily. Just as we should discipline the buffalo with a whip, we must discipline our thoughts. A disciplined mind is like a white buffalo in an open field, pure and calm. No longer hidden, it has matured to the full mastery of itself. Having reached such a state, the buffalo would not leave even if we tried to drive it away. At this point the awakened nature of the Mind is ever-present.

The Mind is constantly in a state of emptiness, being egoless, pure and awake. The Mind of true emptiness manifests the causes and conditions of the present reality; the Mind then acts accordingly, without ego. To act without ego is the perfection of liberation. As long as we maintain the emptiness, awakened nature and clarity of the Mind and act accordingly, there is nothing we cannot let go. We must maintain, in every moment, this bliss, freedom, auspiciousness and tranquility. No merit will exceed our reach.

The Mind is alive and alert. It is capable of any function and can create any appearance. However, the attainment of Mind can only be realized through enlightenment. In this state, the mind is completely pure and in full mastery of itself, whereupon we can create great manifestations in every moment of reality. The pure Mind thus revealed is Buddha, being capable of great achievement and creation to benefit all sentient beings. The egoless Mind is the most powerful, "performing grand Buddhist ceremony in the dream, hosting an elaborate banquet in the hall of forms" and generating the most active functions from the egoless emptiness, ceaselessly liberating sentient beings.

Cultivation must, from the beginning to the end, be centered on the true understanding and application of the nature of the Mind. Any deviation from this is like the script and act of a drama. Reincarnation, then, is an example of a drama. The opposite of this, the result of realizing the principles of the nature of the Mind, is liberation.

Vexation should serve as a sign that we need to reflect upon our karma. Frequent encounters with irritating people and experiences indicate that our negative habits are deeply rooted and our belief and understanding have been poisoned. It is time to reflect; to ask ourselves why we manifest this life and have such habits. We must search for the answers within but not seek them in others.

The first stage of Zen practice is to understand the principles of the nature of the Mind. The second stage is to immerse oneself in the principles and become familiar with them. The third stage requires us to apply the principles in daily life as we train and restrain the habitual tendencies of the mind. Enlightenment will take place when the timing, proper causes and supportive factors all mature: That is the fourth stage. The fifth stage is when one rests at ease in the Dao. This is when we find true refuge. Thus matured, we obtain liberation and nirvana and are able to manifest great functions and beneficial activities. The tenth stanza of the Ox Herding Pictures describes the process this way: "Falling into the dust world with unkempt appearance, the enlightened one keeps a smiling face, although covered with dirt. Unarmed with any secret teaching from immortals, the enlightened one brings withered trees back to life."

Sitting on a prayer cushion I meditate full-heartedly;
when traveling on a pilgrimage, I see men of yesterday
busy with hustle and bustle.
What they learn is nothing but hearsay;
how can it be any match for seeing my own intimate nature.

# 4 REGRESSION IS PROGRESS AFTER ALL

Snow falls and piles up on the peak of the mountain;
two or three pines are the only green in sight.
The hidden message has long been leaked;
even the scriptures have been burned to ashes.

## Liberation Is Letting Go

The goals of Buddhist practice are to achieve liberation, attain the Dao, separate ourselves from suffering and attain enlightenment. Everyone, in fact, should seek liberation. This is not just for practitioners of religion or students of spiritual teachings. The true significance of liberation is to let go; to elevate one's life and become free of all predicaments.

If there is vexation in the mind, freedom is attained by letting go of the vexation. Similarly, when one is sick a kind of freedom is obtained by getting rid of the pain. It is also a liberating experience to escape from financial troubles or problematic relationships. There are many types and degrees of freedom, so there is no need to probe the concept specifically. Unless we attain liberation, difficulties, vexation, suffering and illusions will follow us. Liberation, therefore, should be the goal for each and every one of us. Cultivation is for the purpose of letting go of vexation, attachment, pain and conflict. It is intended to help us live better lives. The goals of spiritual cultivation and worldly pursuit are the same.

People tend to believe spiritual liberation has little to do with them because the problems and vexations in their present lives are more urgent. They will say, "I have no money. I am sick, and I have all sorts of problems. So, I have no time or energy to practice meditation and study the spiritual teachings." However, our current predicament is our karma; we must identify its cause and eliminate the result from its cause. Generally speaking, all issues in this world result from a lack of wisdom and merit. The absence of wisdom and merit causes disease, financial problems, strained relationships, a confused perception of situations, hasty reactions and various negative side effects.

Difficulty in life indicates that a person lacks wisdom and merit. These qualities, however, will develop when the mind becomes increasingly pure and compassionate. Cultivation is for the purpose of resolving our problems and difficulties, which we must do in order to attain complete freedom. Thus, when there are difficulties we should put forth even more effort to adjust the mind. This is the fundamental practice for solving our worldly troubles.

Money solves the issue of a lack of money; good health ends the suffering caused by disease; and a mind free of greed, anger and delusion eliminates the corresponding karma. Remember, liberation is not unreachable. Actually, it is quite close at hand. To become liberated is to let go of negative karma and instead create positive karma. One could equate liberation to death, in which case we mean the death of vexation, difficulty and reincarnation rather than physical death.

We must rely on the correct principles in order to correct our improper thoughts and behaviors. First, we must eliminate our deeply rooted bad habits before we can successfully change our behavior and produce the right result. Adjust your mind now, and you will have a better future. Even if you are in a pretty good situation, you can get even better, relatively speaking. Contrastingly, a lack of effort in the present can allow your good situation to become an obstacle to future improvement. Therefore, whether you are in good shape or poor shape, you should start making an effort.

Cultivation does not mean giving up all worldly business. On the contrary, we must proactively face and resolve the various issues that occur in life. Naturally, a mind that is calm and peaceful brings forth wisdom, merit and positive karma, while a mind that is disturbed and impure brings conflict, chaos and turmoil to the world. This is not some mysterious knowledge or fairy tale, it is the truth. The key is to keep your mind calm. A mind that is free of attachment and vexation will gradually manifest pure merit. The deliberate pursuit of merit does not guarantee results, but a calm, pure mind and correct behavior do.

Attachments in the mind make progress difficult to achieve, but attachment can be eliminated through determination when one aspires to discern the truth. Attachment to one particular thing can only bring suffering, but letting go of such attachment brings freedom. Compared to ancient people, modern men are less diligent, less faithful and less receptive to the truth. Therefore, people suffer more from karma. However, one should always remember that practice takes place in the details of daily life. From the perspective of training the mind, it makes little difference if we practice in a temple or in the context of our worldly affairs.

The ancient people compared spiritual cultivation to the planting of rice sprouts backward: "Hand planting young and green rice sprouts, I lower my head and see the reflection of the sky in the watery rice field. When six roots are pure, the Dao reveals; although walking backward, one actually makes progress." The mind is like a portion of a rice field, and one thought is like a rice sprout that one plants in the mind. The mind, however, is the source and the destination of each thought. When a thought is generated, it is like a rice sprout that takes root in the mind, growing gradually.

The planting of rice sprouts requires walking backward. Similarly, purifying your mind requires self-reflection. "I lower my head and see the reflection of the sky in the watery rice field." When one lowers the head and looks, the water of the rice field reflects the sky; when we look inward and reach the root of a thought, the blue sky of our mind is revealed.

Reflect on the origin of thought, the origin of behavior, the origin of karma and the origin of problems. Why do we encounter these sufferings? It is because we have certain thoughts, personalities and behaviors. You might ask, "Why do I have these thoughts, this personality and these behaviors?" Answer yourself thus: "Because my habits, attachments, pride and forces of negativity, such as greed, anger and delusion, compel me to think and behave that way." Layer by layer, we penetrate the mind through reflection. Eventually, we get to the roots of our issues and resolve them.

Spiritual work requires a person to lower his head and look at himself instead of simply looking at others. It is you, not others, for whom improvement is needed. Without the inspection of our thoughts, behavior and karma, we cannot understand why things are the way they are. We must understand the origin of thoughts— the true face of the Mind essence—in order to see the cause and effect in everything.

Thoughts are generally related to our attachments, even though we are not aware of this relationship. When a thought arises, we believe it and use it. We will follow the same pattern to generate more, similar thoughts. As an ancient saying puts it, "A rumor spread by one person is untrue; the same rumor spread by ten thousand people becomes true." When everyone says the same thing, a falsehood can be accepted as a truth. Unless we can catch thoughts and stop the continual arising, thoughts will occupy our mind and spread similar thoughts until we believe them wholeheartedly.

Similar thoughts accumulate into habits that are nearly impossible to change unless we are equipped with great awareness and make a great effort. For example, you would probably become upset if I were to describe a favorite food of yours as disgusting. After all, it has been your favorite for a long time. Your favorable conclusion about the food's taste is a result of repeated thoughts and experiences. Repeated thoughts are reinforced and entrenched, and they continually drive the situation in the corresponding direction.

A thought appears, but the true practitioner lets it go because he knows it is irrelevant to merit, wisdom and liberation. The practitioner realizes that such thoughts are harmful to the mind. Thoughts of attachment and negativity are poisonous. Continuous, negative thoughts are the poison we feed ourselves. When we continue poisoning ourselves, eventually the tainted mind becomes incurable.

"Purify the six roots of the Dao." The six roots are the eyes, ears, nose, tongue, body and mind. To purify the six roots is to let go of the concept of "I." Truth can only be seen in the absence of self-attachment. When we cling to the concept of "I," we see only our thoughts and opinions. When we let go of "I," our eyes can see, our ears can hear and the mind becomes calm and pure, like the void. A mind filled with ego and judgmental opinions is like an unclean bowl that gets more so with each meal.

The control of the six senses requires us to be mindful of every single thought that arises and refrain from following it with similar ones. If the situation is already troublesome, what good does it do to continually generate negative thoughts? If we are unaware of our thoughts and let our senses grasp the external stimulation, we will gradually but unconsciously develop more and more attachments.

Only a calm mind has the capacity to resolve difficulties and find new opportunities in life. Reality is ever-present. Its existence is due to karma, as a consequence of our thoughts and actions. We can give many reasons for getting sick, such as that we have eaten spoiled food. Eating is an action driven by one's mind, so it has a correlation to getting sick. However, our thoughts and actions are the real causes of illness and disease.

Every consequence has its cause, which is in turn the direction of the mind and its function. Thus the critical solution to worldly suffering is to be aware of our thoughts. Accordingly, we must adjust our minds and let go of attachment. Most people blindly follow their thoughts as they continuously arise in the consciousness. They speak, act and believe, and in the process their minds are flooded with thoughts.

The volume of water at the source of the Yangtze, or the Yellow River, is not great. However, by the time it reaches midstream or downstream there is a vast amount of fast-moving water. Our habitual tendencies behave the same way as the midstream or downstream of a river, with its great momentum. To become aware of our thought is to pay attention to the upstream source of a river; to find the origin of thought and tame it there. The mind's tendency to seek outward is like the flow of a river downstream, as it leads to birth and death. To find the source, we must go against the stream. We must go against the flow of samsara, and therefore regression is actually progress.

We will fail in our mission of elevating life unless we focus our effort on training the mind. If the water at the source of the river is not stopped, once it gains momentum its force can repel any attempt to stop it. Likewise, when faced with a situation the concentration and skills we have acquired through training can suddenly vanish. Until a person practices resting at ease in the essence of the Mind, he has no idea how little mastery he has over his life. Every thought comes from habits and flows forth, outside our conscious control. The true practitioner realizes the destructive power of habitual tendency and the swiftness of karmic forces.

Master Laiguo once said, "Those who know to practice are busy putting an end to birth and death; those who do not busy themselves in their vexation, creating more karma." It takes wisdom and strength to cross the river of samsara. As an ancient saying put it, "One barehandedly forces though the path of samsara and jumps over the Gate of Right and Wrong." To eradicate our wandering thoughts is to open up a path amid the army of vexations. The Gate of Right and Wrong represents duality, because our opinions concerning right and wrong are based on attachment instead of truth. Upon enlightenment, the Mind of the true void reveals itself. It is not about right and wrong or good and evil. Instead, the emptiness, clarity and light transcend our dualistic opinion of reality.

Why do so few of those who study Zen actually end samsara? Why do so few of those who practice truly change themselves? It is because the force of illusion is too strong for the weak mind, and a vulnerable mind cannot find peace. In the past, people endured all sorts of hardships in order to find the Dao, but today people endure hardships in order to accommodate their attachments. For instance, some people would go through a great deal of trouble to fly around the world searching for delicacies. Burdened by illusions and attachments, we become slaves to our desires and negativities.

Spiritual cultivation should be based on the principle of the Mind. The manner in which the Mind functions is the manner in which the result is manifested. We cannot resolve any problem unless we have this basic understanding. The direction of the mind's function determines the corresponding result. From the flower and fruit, we know the seed. When the mind arises, phenomena arise; when the mind vanishes, phenomena vanish. The realm of phenomena turns as the mind turns, and it differs as the mind differs. To change ourselves is to change the world. To solve the problem of life, we must find the problem's root cause.

Appearances change only when we change ourselves. When we increase our recitation from one volume of scripture to three volumes, however, we merely create a change in methodology. It is neither a change in true effort nor the guarantee of a true result. It is a waste of effort to practice without a clear understanding of the issue. Suffering and vexation are caused by the karma we have created. Those who complain about particular phenomena and situations fail to perceive the principle of cause and effect in regard to their problems. A true practitioner, though, looks at his or her own mind. Do not busy yourself with old habits. Instead, focus on the issue of birth and death. Focus on finding the Mind, and you will achieve freedom.

## Cultivation of the Body, Speech and Mind

We, in our ignorance of the concept of elevation, stumble from one obstacle to another, wasting time and energy on insignificant matters. In order to elevate ourselves we must come back to reality. We must examine the basis of our life condition and the foundation upon which we can make improvement. Buddhism refers to the body, speech and mind as the foundation for practice in this life and the result of our past cultivation. We create our present body, speech and mind according to the previous ones, and we create our future body, speech and mind according to the present one.

Dharma is the function and phenomena manifested by the Mind. Because all appearances arise from the Mind, we utilize the phenomena as the tools for elevating life. We use the function of the Mind in the present moment to elevate ourselves. In other words, we use what is false to find what is true. The body, speech and mind are the functions of the Mind, and accordingly they are the vehicle and tools by which we achieve elevation. We have thoughts, so we use thoughts to elevate ourselves. Each of us has a body, which can be utilized in meditation or prostration to elevate ourselves. We can speak, and therefore we can use our voices to spread goodness and truth to help others and ourselves. The most portable and convenient dharma instrument is the proper use of the mind, body and speech. These are collectively the means through which we put the teaching into practice.

People like to rely on things, such as temples, statues of the Buddha, incense offerings, music, tributes and so forth to stimulate introspection. However, our body, speech and mind are the most direct vehicles of dharma. Practice is the transformation of erroneous thinking into proper thinking. Unable to do this, people turn to the study of scriptures and the worship of Buddha figures. They allow the mind to rely on external forms in order to effect the desired change. However, these are not the hallmarks of a genuine practice. Consequently, in a traditional Zen hall there is neither chanting nor prostration practice. Instead, we practice the direct awareness of the mind. We restrain the outward-seeking six senses but inquire into the Mind essence through the vehicles of body, speech and mind.

Attachment to exterior appearances does not help cultivation. Our body, speech and mind are directly manifested by the Mind and are therefore closest to the Mind. The closer we are to the Mind, the more potent a vehicle we become. When meditating, sit straight, ignore any wandering thoughts and scrutinize the innate pureness of the Mind. This is the best way to elevate oneself.

Cultivation is about being aware. It is about changing our thoughts, actions and words. Many so-called practitioners spend considerable time and energy on the external form of the religion but neglect to cultivate the body, speech and mind in life. It is of little benefit to practice only the formality of a religion—the ceremony, the offering and the act of setting up an altar—without cultivation.

A Buddha statue represents the pure Mind. The significance of a Buddha statue is not for the sake of worshiping but instead serves as a reminder of our flaws and the capacity for improvement. Usually, a Buddha statue is placed in the center of a prayer hall to represent the Middle Way. Seeing the thirty-two appearances and eighty wonderful marks of the Buddha, we become aware of our many inner flaws, knowing that "appearance is a manifestation of the Mind" and realizing there is room for improvement. As we perceive the infinite compassion and aspiration of the Buddha, we see our own narrow-mindedness. Through the Buddha statue, we seek to model our lives after the Buddha. We want to correct our personality flaws in order to achieve the merit and wisdom that are most like Buddha.

The significance of the Buddha statue is not as a place to make offerings of incense and water. Instead, it is about the state of mind with which we make the offering. An ordinary mind is filled with illusions and impure thoughts, so it cannot be offered to the true Buddha. However, the manifestation of the pure Mind is a true offering. A water offering reminds us of compassion and the awareness that all beings have the capacity for awakening. A true offering to the Buddha is therefore an offering to all beings. The pure Mind, being free of discrimination, makes the offering to all sentient beings. Water symbolizes purity and gentleness. Such a state of mind is the key to the wisdom that benefits all beings according to their needs.

Because we do not know how to generate thoughts properly, we must first rely on external appearances. We chant because we have not learned how to utter beneficial speech. We think according to the scriptures because we fail to recognize our own flaws. Before we embark upon the spiritual path, we rely on our parents, mentors, friends and books to help us create beneficial thoughts. Once we encounter religious teaching, we begin to make offerings, meditate and read scripture. We start using different tools to train the mind, and a mind thus trained will yield different results. Ultimately, we should know that true practice is nothing other than our body, speech and mind. These are the tools we use to take care of ourselves. If one does not understand this, he or she can chant this moment but curse the next; the same body can meditate this moment but behave badly the next; and the same mind can recite scriptures this moment but create negativity the next. In such a state, spiritual progress is difficult to achieve.

We burn incense for the Buddha statue, but can a statue of bronze or wood smell the scent? It cannot. It is the intention that matters. With the right intention, inferior incense could be offered to Buddha, but with the wrong intention even the finest incense will fail to dispel ignorance and vexation. Everything depends on how the mind functions. The rising smoke of incense symbolizes elevation. It reminds us to become more aware and compassionate with each and every thought.

True practice simply requires the proper use of the body, speech and mind. Master Huisi once said, "The source of Dao is not far; the sea of Buddha nature is not distant." The mind is the source of all life forms. "Just search within; never look elsewhere." The Dao is found within. Everyone possesses a mind that can function and create results. Everyone carries the tools and vehicles of dharma practice. There is no need to look elsewhere.

Pay attention to your thoughts, and you will be on the path to Dao. Otherwise, all appearances will remain illusory. If we focus only on the spiritual method but do not change and elevate our thoughts, such a method and its rituals of practice will be little more than acting, as if in an opera. Methods and practice instruments are convenient means for purifying the mind. The goal, however, is to help us let go of attachment and conflicts, improve our lives and reveal the path to freedom.

## Making Progress, Thought by Thought

The ordinary mind functions according to judgmental opinions, and therefore the human realm is inherently a mixture of good and evil. If the mind functions along the general direction of negativity, we will be chained to the three lower states of existence: hell, demons and beasts. If our mind functions primarily in the direction of benevolence and service, we will be like the heavenly beings. If our mind functions according to the principle of emptiness, clarity, illumination and selflessness, we will walk the path of the saints.

The various paths, thus determined, are inseparable from the Mind. They result from the Mind's functioning.

The things we pursue are usually fickle appearances, which inevitably vanish from our grasp. However, if we realize the original Mind we will then find life's inexhaustible treasure. So, we must carefully consider what we will pursue as a life goal. In the pursuit of enlightenment, we seek to manifest the eternal Mind through the impermanence of the body, speech and mind, because they are our tools for elevating the mind and soul. Although these tools are impermanent, they are our wisest investment when used to elevate the spirit.

Once the mind is pure and calm, it is capable of creating a better reality. At this point, one can have health, a pleasant physical appearance and better relationships. On the contrary, if we pursue impermanent materialism with our impermanent body, speech and mind, life will remain unsettled and subject to upheavals.

If each moment of good thought is followed by another moment of pure, compassionate thought, one is in the process of purification and elevation. If each moment of negative thought is followed by another moment of negative thought such as anger, attachment or vexation, the mind is subject to degeneration. Spiritual work is like climbing stairs: Our present body, speech and mind represent our position on the stairway, where each good thought elevates us upward but a negative one brings us downward. Where we stand right now is the foundation of our practice, and consequently, whether we ascend or descend depends on us.

Zen Master Baizhang, during his boyhood, once visited a Buddhist temple with his mother. He asked his mother to tell him who the center statue was. His mother said it was the Buddha. Young and determined, Baizhang said, "Buddha looks no different from a human being. So, when I grow up I want to be a Buddha." Buddha and the saints were initially men, and likewise our destiny depends on the path we pave for ourselves. Spiritual work requires not only great determination but also cautious work. The most solid practice is the one that is able to eradicate vexation, attachment and bad habits. Habits are not created in one day, so they cannot be eliminated with one stroke. As soon as we sense that our thoughts are deviating, we must rein them back and control them.

The highest achievement of spiritual cultivation is to recognize the innate Mind, because "any dharma that is proclaimed to surpass nirvana is illusion." Therefore, nirvana is the empty nature of the Mind. A mind that is free of ego is also free of attachment. The function of such a mind disappears as soon as it is created. Birth and death are simultaneous, but birth and death are inseparable. To recognize the Mind is to wipe away any blemish that defiles the mind in order to reveal its innate nature. Master Mazu once said, "Dao requires no cultivation; all one needs to do is to keep it from being polluted." A mind that is not polluted naturally manifests the Dao. The polluted mind is the way of most people, and it is the woeful realm of reincarnation.

Zen is great, but can Zen study ever surpass the nature of the innate Mind? It cannot. The purpose of Zen is to eradicate attachment, illusion and ignorance so as to reveal the nature of the Mind. It is said that tantric empowerment is so unique that it surpasses the Mind, but this is impossible. The most supreme dharma is the pure Mind. With a pure Mind, every word we utter is as powerful as a mantra. If the mind is impure, every incantation uttered remains polluted.

The Mind cannot be surpassed by Buddhism, whether it is Mahayana, Esoteric or Theravada, because the Mind is the nature of nirvana. A polluted mind will become attached to certain appearances and thus develop preferences. Modern people are intrigued by mysterious practices or teachings, but the mystery one perceives in something is merely a creation of the Mind and is therefore subject to dissolution. The highest dharma, both spiritually and worldly, is the eternal, pure, egoless innate Mind. It is the essence worth learning and understanding.

The Mind is innately pure. Therefore, once it is realized everything will become pure as the manifestation of Buddha. It is impractical—even futile—to practice without purifying ourselves and our minds. When the mind is free, all phenomena are liberated as well. Spiritual cultivation is the process of elevating ourselves thought by thought, like ascending stairs through the concerted practice of a method. When we reach the stage where there are steps every moment but also the absence of steps in every moment, we achieve freedom from reincarnation. The cause is inseparable from the consequence. Matter and principle, existence and emptiness, Mind and Buddha are all inseparable.

"The unborn-ness of prior thought is inseparable from the Mind; the deathlessness of the next thought is inseparable from the Buddha." The idea of inseparability or immediacy means something is right as truth and is used appropriately. Whether the Mind functions with or without ego, it creates appearances. "Mind and Buddha are inseparable" refers to the function of the Mind. The "function of the pure Mind" is dharma. The function of the pure Mind is such that phenomena are present without ego. This peace in the mind is the "unborn-ness of prior thought," or the inseparability of the Mind. In other words, while all phenomena are egoless or selfless, all phenomena are of the self. The essence of the pure Mind is emptiness with infinite potential. The "deathlessness of the next thought" means the Mind is omnipotent and complete in itself. It is the Buddha.

"Inseparability," or immediacy, means that phenomena cannot be separated from their essence. The essence, function and form of the Mind are inseparable. When the Mind functions, there is form and there is function. These are inseparable from the Mind. In the instant of the Mind function, there is a true void without self or any distinction between the inner and the outer. Therefore, it is inseparable from the Buddha. In this very instance, there is no prior thought or next thought. It is for the sake of convenience that we call the function of the Mind "prior thought" and refer to the function of a selfless Mind as the "next thought." The present Mind manifests all phenomena but does so without attachment, because it rests in innate emptiness. This is the inseparability of Mind and Buddha. It is the inseparability of emptiness and existence, the non-duality of Mind and Buddha, and the non-duality of emptiness and existence.

Spiritual work is the wise utilization of our impermanent body, speech and mind in order to continuously elevate ourselves. We do this work in order to reach the state of true liberation, in which

Mind and Buddha are inseparable. Everyone has a unique dharma instrument that comprises the body, speech and mind, as well as the most direct practice of introspection in the mind. When we are not able to practice introspection, we rely on Zen inquiry, mantra practice, chanting and prostration, as well as various religious methods to eliminate attachment and achieve the goal of liberation.

Master Baizhang plows the field deeply
and plants seeds of merit to benefit us descendents.
I light an incense to pay tribute to the ancestral master,
praying for one harvest year after another.

# **5** FACE THE PRESENT LIFE

Green water, high waves, the Mind is calm;

each camellia in my courtyard is unique.

Passing by a busy market, I see a multitude of pure palaces;

although decorated with stone lions, the palaces have few

traces of inhabitants.

## No Explanation Can Surpass the Fact

We should focus our efforts on the Mind because, if used without understanding, it becomes the source of vexation. As the saying goes, "Everyone uses the Mind without understanding it." The Mind is formless, but through direct realization we will know what the Mind is.

The Zen poems of the "Ten Ox Herding Pictures" illustrate the ten stages one goes through from initial training to enlightenment. The ordinary human mind is like a wild ox: untrained, chaotic and troubled with conflicts. Unlike a tamed ox, which can be employed for farming and productive labor, an untrained ox can trample and destroy crops because it is ignorant, ill-tempered and burdened by vexation.

One must train an ox before he can put it to work. The wild nature of the beast must be tamed, or it will not only consume food without being productive but may also damage crops or even human lives. Similarly, when a person's mind is filled with vexation, illusion, attachment and judgmental opinions, he or she will pass the days consuming food and other resources without engaging in any productive work. Consider it for a moment, and you will see that many people live this way.

We can try monitoring our thoughts with a scientific method. Carry a little notebook with you at all times, and make an entry whenever a negative thought appears. This way, you can track how many negative thoughts are generated each day. The Mind is our own and the thoughts are our own, so we cannot avoid the responsibility for any predicament we face in life.

Intellectual explanations such as "impermanence" or "dependent origination" are meaningless to those who, through genuine effort, face their own vexations and attachments. One can say that vexation and attachment are of impermanence and therefore void, but can we actually let them go? We cannot. If you do not even know where thoughts come from, how can you let them go? Many people are taught these concepts but cannot apply even one of them to reality. In such cases, the concepts are useless in the effort to elevate our lives.

Set aside all principles and ideas, and know this basic fact: We can generate thoughts, but each negative thought creates negative energy, poor facial features and an unpleasant atmosphere. This is the bare fact. All the other sayings are just explanations. To say thoughts come from the Mind is an explanation, and to say thoughts disappear the moment they appear is another explanation. To say the Mind generates thoughts due to attachment is an explanation, and to say thoughts are results of various conditions coming together is another explanation. Can these explanations actually change us?

Principles are used to explain what facts are and how they

come into being, but no principle can replace the fact. Therefore, spiritual cultivation should be based on the fundamental facts of the present moment but not on the intellectual understanding of principles. For now, we should ignore whether our ability to think comes from God or Buddha, or whether it is innate. As long as we have our thoughts, appearance, body and relationships, we must be responsible for them.

Spiritual work requires self-responsibility. Spiritual truths are goals to be achieved but not simply for the purpose of intellectual explanation. Spiritual truth is based on the direct realization of enlightened beings; the scriptures and recorded sayings are their thoughts, not yours. Therefore, quoting them in an effort to explain phenomena can be considered borrowing ideas or even plagiarism and misuse.

Consider a subtler koan: Elder Muzhou once said to a monk who had recently arrived at his temple, "How can you steal fruit here? You are a monk. Why do you not observe the five precepts? The five precepts are 'no killing, no stealing, no adultery, no lies and no intoxicants.'" At that moment, the monk was standing in the middle of the hall; he had nothing in his hands. He was utterly shocked that the master had accused him of telling lies and stealing.

Any function or appearance manifested by the Mind disappears instantaneously, but an unenlightened person with an unclear mind tends to cling to previous thoughts and situations. Therefore, it is a form of theft to function without letting go. This is what Elder Muzhou meant in the koan. Any function of the Mind appears, exists and vanishes instantaneously. Any grasping means the "theft-mind" has not subsided.

The present reality is the way it is for a reason. Therefore, reality emerges according to certain underlying principles, and the underlying principles are illustrated through the present reality. Thus the manifested reality and underlying principles are as one. They are inseparable. Only the principle that underlies the present manifestation is the true principle. However, the principles people deduce from present facts are usually not consistent with those that support the facts.

A dharma teacher who specialized in the Huayen Sutra paid a visit to Master Qi'an. Master Qi'an asked him how many dharma realms there were in the Huayen Sutra. The teacher explained that there are four realms: the non-obstructive principle realm, non-obstructive phenomenal realm, non-obstructive between principle and phenomena realm, and the non-obstructive among the phenomena realm. Hearing this, Master Qi'an waved his duster and asked, "To which dharma realm does this belong?" The visiting monk was speechless, as he was unable to explain the present moment's reality with his intellectual understanding of the principles.

It would be quite a success if we could realize the principles from the facts of our lives. However, it is a failure not to match our lives with understanding. It is a fact that when we are seated, practicing, the whole time our bodies are changing; hence the impermanence. The limitless energy forms endless new combinations, hence the dependent origination. The boundless energy of the Mind overlaps time and space, hence the Huayen realms. As we sit here, our minds function through a certain discriminating consciousness, and this is the function of the Mind-Only principle.

Life is a fact as well as a principle. The fact that we sit in practice is the manifestation of impermanence, dependent origination, the principle that functions arise from the Mind, the principle of the Huayen, Tientai and Mind-Only teachings. Even our sitting alone can be expounded upon endlessly, because it is the manifestation of these principles. Principles are not found in the scripture alone, nor can the principles in the scripture surpass the fact that we sit in the present moment.

Life manifests and directly explains the most supreme principle of existence. If the facts did not match the principles, our spiritual work would be more difficult. We would not really understand what life is, nor would we appreciate the usefulness of understanding the principles. However, if we can use the fact in every moment of life and harmonize with the principles we have learned, we will become more aware and possess the right understanding; we will know the principles behind our behaviors and phenomena. The facts and principles will become integrated in our understanding.

Thoughts and actions are manifestations of truth. Do you believe that vexation reflects truth? It does, actually. There is vexation because there is the Mind, able to function in various ways and lead to different appearances. Therefore, the manifestation of vexation is also a manifestation of the truth. The Zen masters were not talking nonsense when they said, "Dao is in pee and poo." Every moment of life reflects the truth, so there is no truth that is separate from the reality of life. Truth is neither sentimental nor biased with judgments of right and wrong. A person, whether good or bad, can generate thoughts. It is a universal truth that each of us has the ability to function with the Mind. We should practice in order to see things through this principle.

## You Would Know Only After Your Destination Is Reached

The monk Shuigun, in paying his respects to Master Mazu, asked, "What is the true meaning of the teaching that came from the West?" Mazu said, "Now kowtow!" So, the monk Shuigun started kowtowing to Master Mazu, who, with the stamping of feet, forced him to the ground. Shuigun was instantly enlightened. He stood up, laughing and saying, "How strange! How strange! The secret of thousands of Buddhist teachings, the source of all, is revealed at the tip of a hair!" How can the tip of a hair surpass all the marvelous teachings of the Buddha? If you reach the state where the masters are, you will understand; otherwise, you will have no clue.

Scriptures and treatises capture the understanding of the Buddha and ancestral masters. They speak the truth only after reaching that state of understanding. Therefore, we must be cautious when borrowing their ideas because we do not understand as they do. It is foolish to speak all day of emptiness despite being troubled by vexation, attachment and illusion and avoiding our reality. Real cultivation means becoming aware of our thoughts and being able to dissolve negativities in order to purify our thoughts, personality and behaviors.

The purification of our mind and actions is not necessarily related to the practices of meditation, chanting and incantation. It depends on how we apply these things. For example, if we meditate with negative motivations and thoughts on hatred, anger and delusion, the outcome of our meditation will not be what we desire. Thus the duration of meditation is not the only important aspect; more important is the question of whether we have clear, correct awareness. Only a pure mind that manifests the right thoughts, combined with prolonged meditation, will be helpful.

Zen koans are composed of simple questions and answers, because every moment of life is an embodiment of truth. The Zen masters understand and are able to use life's principle with liveliness and spontaneity. Each moment—every gesture—is an opportunity to reveal the truth without deliberate pondering. For example, if you were to ask about the oneness of emptiness and existence, I would slap you. If you were well prepared and ready to see the truth, you would understand the oneness of emptiness and existence in the slapping. Otherwise, you would think I was insane for striking you randomly.

Set aside what you have learned or heard, and face yourself in order to see where you stand. Do not allow religious study to stupefy you, so that you know all kinds of spiritual principles but are unable to apply any of them in real life. Do not be burdened by the weight of vexation and attachment while continuing to think highly of your intellectual understanding.

Do not cling to ideas you have acquired and think of them as your own. In the absence of true understanding, this is the same as stealing. Do not carry around what you steal on your shoulders and brag about it, because it will be quite obvious. A spiritual understanding is yours only when you can apply it and accomplish it in life. Before reaching the peak of the mountain, you cannot describe to others what it is like to be at the top. You never see the actual picture by hearing descriptions from others. Only when you reach the top can you draw a conclusion.

"The human mind is like a wild ox that must be tamed." Therefore, we must look after the mind. Once we find this ox, it must be tamed. Even after we attain enlightenment, we must continue to care for our minds. Zen does not indulge in theoretical elaborations such as the question, "What is Buddha nature, impermanence or dependent origination?" Instead, it illustrates the truth through very simple analogies: If the mind is like a wild ox, can you look after it? Can your mind create thoughts? If so, are you in charge of which thought you want to create? The answer is probably, "No." Because the thoughts are yours, the ox is yours. Therefore, you must take responsibility for the unwieldy behavior of the ox.

You know there is an ox wandering nearby if you see the hoof prints. Similarly, if you are aware of your thoughts but cannot identify who is creating them, you must first determine the source. Once you eradicate all attachments and reach enlightenment, the source—the true you—will be revealed. Even then, in order to employ the ox in farming and pulling cargo, you must continuously work to tame the ox and keep it so.

Most spiritual practitioners only understand, in a theoretical way that vexation results from the function of the Mind. They have not yet found the Mind. Despite the fact they have not found the Mind, they use it whenever they hear, think, see and generate thoughts. These are the marks of the untamed ox. Nevertheless, such functions are the hoof prints of the ox that will eventually lead to enlightenment.

Master Fachang asked Master Mazu to describe Buddha. Mazu replied, "The Mind is Buddha." Master Fachang then took up this principle as his basis for the practice of Zen. After a few years, Mazu sent a disciple to test Master Fachang and tell him that Master Mazu's teaching had become different because it was "neither Buddha nor the Mind." In response, Master Fachang said, "Master Mazu is confusing and misleading people. I do not care what his teaching is. As far as I am concerned, the Mind is Buddha." After hearing the report, Mazu said, "The plum has ripened."

The lay Buddhist Pangyun, having heard Master Fachang's story, decided to pay a visit and examine the master's level of spiritual realization. At that meeting, Pangyun asked, "I have long heard of you. Has the plum ripened or not?" Fachang replied, "Yes, it has. From which part of it would you have a bite?" Pangyun said, "I will eat it in a hundred pieces." Master Fachang extended one hand, saying, "Give me the pit." Pangyun was speechless.

Master Fachang recognized and rested in the pure Mind, so he was able to affirm the true self. If you could reach such a stage, you would no longer be confused and misled by the teachings of monks from older days. Before getting there, you would blindly follow various forms and sayings, but you would not be able to understand the subtle meaning of a koan. You would instead become lost, as if wandering helplessly through mile after mile of fog. "How could a mosquito manage to bite an iron ox?" This ancient saying describes the lack of a leverage point for the practice. You know that a principle underlies the koan, but despite any effort you are unable to figure it out. As long as you fail to identify the innate Mind, you will find no leverage or entry point to the truth. Therefore, you will tend to read scriptures between the lines and become overly analytical. With a mind dulled by attachments, a person is easily moved by various sayings.

## Buddha Nature Is About Taking Responsibility

Spiritual cultivation is based on the acknowledgment of the principle that the Mind is Buddha, so Buddhahood requires that one be fully responsible for his or her mind. For example, Master Huilang paid a visit to Master Mazu. Mazu asked him, "What are you here for?" Huilang said, "I am here to pursue Buddha's knowledge." Mazu replied, "Buddha has no knowledge. Only demons have it."

Why would he say only demons have knowledge? As the scriptures explain, "Knowledge that is built upon discriminating consciousness is the root of ignorance." The Mind is not restrained by specific ideas, because it can generate anything and everything. Prior to enlightenment, your mind has not reached the state of true emptiness, awareness and wisdom, and consequently your belief that "the Mind can generate anything and everything" is merely conceptual. It is a kind of attachment that you form out of the emptiness nature of your mind and then try to grasp. Accordingly, it is the knowledge of demons. So, is it correct to state that "the Mind can generate anything and everything?" It depends on who says it. If an enlightened being says it, it is Buddha's knowledge; if an unenlightened being says it, it is demons' knowledge. Enlightenment makes all the difference.

Master Huilang could not understand when Master Mazu said there is no Buddha knowledge but only demons' knowledge. So, Mazu then asked him, "Where are you from?" He replied, "From Nanyue." Mazu asked, "Coming from Nanyue, why do you not know the Caoxi principles?" Caoxi is where the Sixth Patriarch began his Zen teaching, and thus the Caoxi principles refer to the Sixth Patriarch's teachings of the Mind.

Mazu told Huilang to go directly back to Master Shitou. Empowered with strong Zen insight, Mazu knew the trigger for Huilang's enlightenment was with Master Shitou, who lived in Nanyue and had obtained great wisdom. To put it simply, there is a place with abundant fire; but instead of going there for fire, you look elsewhere, so of course you cannot find fire.

It was a double meaning when Mazu reminded Huilang to go back to Nanyue. To go back to where one comes from means one returns to the Mind. Because the Mind is where function arises, of course it is the only place to which one can return.

Huilang went back to Master Shitou and asked, "What is Buddha?" Master Shitou replied, "You have no Buddha nature." Huilang was surprised by the seemingly irrelevant answer, as if to say, "I asked you what Buddha is, but you reply that I do not have Buddha nature?" Similarly, if you ask me a question I would reply that you are not "you." You would probably be stunned and could only wonder about what I have said.

Confused, Huilang asked, "Then, how do you explain that all

creatures have Buddha nature?" Master Shitou replied, "All creatures indeed have Buddha nature." Huilang further asked, "If that is true, why do I have no Buddha nature?" Master Shitou said, "It is because you would not take the responsibility." Upon hearing this, Huilang was enlightened.

You have no Buddha nature because you are not willing to take responsibility for your entire karma, including your appearance, relationships, thoughts and life experience, all of which are of your mind's creation. We should abide by this recognition. To achieve any accomplishment through spiritual cultivation, we must endure hardship, which is not that of physical pain in meditation but that of dissolving vexation. We naturally avoid hardships, but spiritual cultivation means hardship because we have to face our negativities. Therefore, we must change for the better. If not, we will suffer the consequences and inflict pain on others in our lives.

Be responsible for your mistakes and troubles, but accept the fact that change is gradual. Do not be concerned that your progress is slow, but instead be concerned only about the temptation to avoid reality. People often say, "It's not my problem." The refusal to acknowledge our problems means there is no progress. Is it not a contradiction when we refuse to accept our problems but continue to be troubled by them?

One does not need an abundance of principles. Simply focus on transforming thoughts and letting go of attachments. If you can do it, the truth is yours; if you cannot, it is not yours. People of ancient times talked about the stage of no regression, and it referred to the stage where one achieved enlightenment and could therefore rest.

Nowadays, many spiritual seekers do not cultivate themselves the right way, and consequently they stagnate. I refer to this as the stage of no regression. They do not make progress, so there is no room for regression.

If no progress is made in understanding the principles after practicing for five or ten years, how does one expect to have proper action? Proper action cannot take place without an understanding of the function and nature of the Mind. Practice identifying your vexation and attachment, focus on your mind, return to the Mind through its various functions, and you will find the "ox." After finding the ox, one must continue his cultivation in the details of daily life so as not to lose focus amid various situations.

> High mountains, cold water, the breeze blows
> and reveals a lotus flower;
> I am just about to ask a question

> but the lotus flower vanishes.
> An appearance in an abandoned thatched cottage
> magically emerges;
> With great dignity he points out for me the red lotus.

# 6 THE WISDOM OF THE NON-DUALITY OF MIND AND MATTER

A sudden breeze gives me a chill as I walk by the
willow trees around the lake.
"Di-da-la, di-da-la, dic," go the falling drops from the bridge,

 stroking my ears.

As I pass by the staggered ox cart on the path,
When nature is simply doing its work, what can we blame for
the afflictions along the way?

## True Peace Comes with Awareness

Buddhism emphasizes the attainment of wisdom, and wisdom is attained through the arising of awareness. This state of awakening dispels illusions and our grasping at surface appearances, and therefore it puts an end to repeated suffering. Buddha is one who awakens to the innate Mind and the knowledge that all things are temporal, being created by the Mind. There is no need to pursue external phenomena, because they stand where the Mind does. To rest in the innate Mind's pure, egoless essence gives rise to wisdom because the mind is no longer confused by phenomena.

The innate Mind, which is free of ego, has no physical form. However, it has the everlasting function of creating all phenomena. Its eternal nature is described in the Heart Sutra as "neither rising nor ceasing." Meanwhile, the actualization and spirituality that we can gain by rediscovering the innate Mind are not tangible; such attainment is recognized only after a person has achieved that rediscovery. Ancient wisdom teaches that the innate Mind is "gained from where there is no gaining." Therefore, attaining the Way is like listening to a speech. As the sounds of the speech travel to the listener, he or she will not be able to catch or keep those sounds but they are clearly heard without effort. This principle is demonstrated through the metaphor of a standing mirror. The mirror reflects images without a "self" identity. It merely reflects what is, without a trace of its own presence.

The Zen practitioner should focus on breaking the ego attachment before attempting to recover the innate Mind. Ego is the manifestation of a mind that functions while grasping its own creation in daily life, and in the human being it operates anytime and anywhere. We must pay close attention to our state of mind at all times, so as to reduce and eliminate the influence of the ego. To attain the Way, we must cultivate ourselves in everyday actions.

Enlightenment is attained when the ego attachment is broken. When a practitioner rests at ease with the emptiness, awareness and light of the innate Mind, he functions without the separation between self and others. He cultivates positive actions without the attachment of selfishness. Now, all phenomena manifest through the law of cause and effect without ego conflict, and this is how the Pure Land is established. However, when the Mind is influenced by the ego, duality arises through the opposition between the self and the external world: the duality of right now, and of birth and death. This is the defiled land. It is a contaminated world.

The innate Mind has not arisen in dependence upon other

things. It exists independently. Thus the innate Mind can manifest phenomena, but nothing was ever born in the first place. This is transcendental manifestation. Having realized the innate Mind, the practitioner will understand that it is existence but empty, and that it is emptiness but exists. Therefore, life is boundless. This is not a philosophical point but a truth that can be actualized. Only when we put an effort into actualizing this dharma can we gain faith and understanding.

One must practice in order to transcend attachment to the ever-changing mind and reach a full realization of the Mind. The ego is ever-changing. To abandon it, you must let go of worldly matters and all dharma. Breaking through ego is like opening up the cloud to reveal the moon, whereupon the awakened nature of the Mind shines through. What you learn from the Buddha is to be awake. All practice is useless if you stray from this, regardless of how knowledgeable you might be in the scriptures and the teachings of saints. The wrong concept, wrong method and wrong conduct will prevent you from reaching your spiritual goal.

Zen Master Yangshan, of the Tang Dynasty, cut off two fingers to show his courage and determination to become a monk when his parents refused to let him leave home and enter the Way. He was just fourteen years old. Later, he attained his awakening and opened a dharma hall in order to teach the Way. One day, a monk from India descended from the sky to request his teaching of the dharma. Master Yangshan asked, "Where are you from?" The Indian monk responded, "The west." "When did you leave from there?" "This morning." Master Yangshan exclaimed, "What a latecomer!" The monk then explained that he had gallivanted around before reaching the monastery. Master Yangshan asserted, "Supernatural power you certainly have. However, when it comes to the Buddha dharma, only I have." The Indian monk praised him in amazement, saying, "I made this special trip to the eastern land to pay homage to Manjushri, but to my surprise I meet a little Sakyamuni Buddha instead." To show appreciation for the teaching, the monk gave the master the Sanskrit scriptures he had brought, whereupon he flew away. Ever since then, Master Yanghan was nicknamed "Little Sakya."

Many practitioners who have read this koan wonder if it is true that a man could fly. They indulge in the speculation instead of focusing on practicing the message in the teaching. Too often practitioners impose their worldly understanding and deluded interpretations on the teaching and believe this is spiritual practice. There was a longtime lay practitioner who could meditate for four to five hours at a time. His understanding of the power of "supernatural foot" is that whatever one thinks of will immediately be manifested. This is the wrong concept. The supernatural foot is a power whereby the physical body can go anywhere the thoughts go. This is one of six possible supernatural powers that arise with spiritual practice. Even non-Buddhist practitioners or those who are not yet enlightened may attain this ability. This power is also available to the spirits, or the heavenly beings. However, the highest supernatural power is the Dao, which is eternal and innate to the original, pure Mind.

If you do not believe in supernatural powers, you should refrain from any conclusion regarding the matter instead of simply denying the possibility that such powers exist. There are many things that mankind does not yet understand, and there is plenty of room for mankind to grow. Flexibility and receptiveness or, as taught by Confucianism, "no speculation, no forced conclusion, no stubbornness, no self-righteousness," also constitute a form of spiritual practice.

One must possess wisdom, the faculty for wholesomeness and merit in order to encounter and trust the truth. Many people run around and work hard in their daily lives, but they constantly suffer from worldly pains. However, when they are taught the way of escape from afflictions they are unwilling to listen. Nevertheless, they try to tell others how to escape their afflictions. Such people lack sufficient merit and wisdom, and they tend to bring suffering to themselves and others.

How did Zen Master Yangzhan reach the conclusion that the Indian monk had supernatural power but had not attained the dharma? This was revealed in the first answer the monk gave Master Yangshan when asked where he came from. The monk replied, "The west." Buddhism teaches the non-duality of mind and matter. Clearly you are here right now, so where is the west anyway? It is only the attachment in the mind that believes one comes from somewhere else. The truth is, with a single movement of thought the world moves too. The world moves with the mind.

Based on the same principle, the monk's answer revealed his lack of wisdom regarding the truth when he said that he had departed for the monastery in the morning. The instant the question is answered is the instant the mind functions. Where the function is, the mind is and the person is. Master Yangshan tried to give him a hint by saying he had arrived too late. Unfortunately, he failed to understand and tried to explain that he was late because he had been touring around. So, finally the Zen master concluded that this monk merely had supernatural powers but had not attained a profound understanding of the truth.

A person who has the correct understanding plants the right seed, which guarantees that, sooner or later, the right fruit will be produced. Contrastingly, when the wrong seed is planted it is useless to spend time and effort on it because it will bring nothing but disappointment and suffering. During the reign of Emperor Huizong, of the Song Dynasty, the villagers of Jiazhou found a man deep in meditative absorption inside a tree that had been uprooted by a storm. So, the villagers carried him into the palace to show the emperor. The dharma master at the palace asked the person to emerge from meditation and identify himself. The man said he was the junior fellow apprentice of Master Weiyun, of the Jin Dynasty, seven hundred years in the past. Emperor Huizong was so impressed with the master's extraordinary concentration in meditation that he ordered the royal painter to draw a portrait of the master, and he then sent copies to temples throughout the land so that all might honor it. A lay practitioner took one such portrait to Zen Master Wanglong Weinan for an inscription, whereupon the master wrote: "Seven hundred years of meditation, confounding the world of sentient beings; without a singular thought stirring, one transcends the limit of time."

Zen Buddhism emphasizes the practice of meditative concentration but not "dead" concentration. In dead concentration, the practitioner can subdue vexation during meditation but is helpless against external phenomena once the meditation ends. Meditation is not a suppression of the senses that stifles the mind's function. Meditation is a state that must be entered. It is a form of birth and death. It cannot transcend the world and get to the root cause of our problems. The focus of meditation is to reveal the wisdom— the awakened nature—and become the master of the mind. It is not about stopping the mind's functions. When the pure Mind and its pure functions are revealed, it naturally responds to the inexhaustible world of phenomena and is able to interact without being corrupted. The true cultivation of concentration is the revelation of the innate Mind's essence and function. This is the meditative concentration that can free us from suffering.

If the mind is pure, one will not be deluded by the world, and therefore concepts such as ego versus the external world or time and space do not exist. The pure Mind is naturally undiluted and free of restrictions. It functions vibrantly and proactively, creating phenomena in the world without being consumed by such phenomena. A Zen master described this state as "walking through a flowering bush without leaving even a leaf on the body." The innate Mind naturally creates phenomena without attachment, reflecting clearly on every matter and every being in the world, like the mirror that is clean and free of dust.

Prime Minister Peixiu, of the Tang Dynasty, once saw a portrait of a Buddhist saint at a temple and asked, "Who is in the picture?" The monk replied, "Grand Master Zhenyi." Prime Minister Peixiu then asked, "The form can be seen, but where is the grand master?" The monk gave no answer. The prime minister then asked, "Is there a Zen practitioner here?" In reply, the monk said, "A traveling monk who recently came to the monastery and is doing labor work appears to practice Zen, if one judges by his behavior."

The prime minister immediately asked to see the monk, who was Zen Master Huangbo. Peixiu asked him the same set of questions, and the master shouted out, "Peixiu!" The prime minister responded. The master continued, "Where are you?" This question enlightened the prime minister instantly. He finally understood that the mind that was asking the question was the Buddha, the true face of the grand master in the painting. The true grand master was an individual person.

Peixiu truly believed in spiritual cultivation. Not only did he work very hard in his practice, but he also sent his son to practice with the grand master Weishan and renounce the ways of secular life. As his son departed on that journey, he composed the following: "The partridges on the sides of the river sobbed, as I sent off my son at the Tiger Stream. When you reach the end of mountain and river, the time is ripe for a transformation." To reach the "end of mountain and river" means the complete eradication of false understanding. Once the mind is purified, the natural aliveness of the original Mind will manifest. This is the transformation.

Persistence is essential if we are to cultivate the mind and forego attachment. The doubtful person has a mind too shallow to actualize the truth, but one who is awakened has a clear mind whose understanding can reach the ultimate level. Consequently, before anyone reaches the highest stage of realization he or she must nurture the ability to distinguish between the dharma and the worldly. The person whose understanding is filled with "maybe," "maybe not," "I probably know" or "I do not think I know" shows that he is not firmly established in the right understanding.

Master Weishan, knowing that Peixiu's son was the preeminent scholar of the Tang Dynasty, wanted to train him. Thus the master sent Peixiu's son down the mountain every day to fetch water. Without understanding that the innate Mind could be rediscovered in daily life, he became fed up with the tedious chore of fetching water and said, "The water fetched by the prestigious scholar is hard for the monk to digest." Master Weishan responded and said, "One meditation by this old monk can digest even a thousand pounds of food."

The ancient saying is as follows: "Without putting an end to the mind of past, present and future, it is impossible to absorb a single drop of nourishment; but with a unified and purified mind, even gold can be transfigured." When the mind creates phenomena, it generates energy. If the mind is diluted by the paradoxes of subject versus object and ego versus "other," the energy not dissolved into the emptiness nature of the essence becomes the deluded sentient being. Without turning discrimination into wisdom, letting go of the three states of mind—namely the grasping of the past, present and future—we will not be able to resolve a single drop of water with reality. Contrastingly, if we return to the essence of the innate Mind we will be able to do much more than digest a thousand pounds of food, as the grand master commanded. Indeed, we will be able to govern the entire universe.

## Buddhist Teaching Transcends Duality

The patriarch said, "If the path in front of us is not recognized, you won't see the road just by walking." In other words, if you do not see that the Mind is already the present moment of reality, you cannot see the non-duality of the Mind and phenomena. If you do not realize the Mind directly, you cannot experience it through the senses such as by seeing or listening.

Dharma combats are traditional in Zen, as are interactions between practitioners based on their experience of the dharma. Worldly debate is based on ego, while dharma debate is a way of testing a practitioner's understanding of the Mind dharma through lively interactions that reveal attachments regarding principles and phenomena. In other words, we test the aliveness and flexibility of one practitioner's mind against another. The Mind is originally alive, flexible and pure, but attachment can prevent the mind from displaying its essential state of freedom. Whether the attachment is in regard to principles or phenomena, it prevents the practitioner from understanding the true meaning of a Zen master's teaching. A person falls in dharma combat because his or her mind cannot turn away from the attachment.

An elder monk called Zhaozhou, a student of Zen Master Puyuan in Nanchuan, once visited Zen Master Daowu. When the master saw him, Master Puyuan immediately said, "Here comes a shooting arrow from Nanchuan!" Elder Zhaozhou, who was very wise and had keen insight, immediately replied, "Watch for the arrow!" Master Puyuan said, "Passed!" implying that words are gone the moment they are spoken. Zhaozhou immediately said, "Hit!" This is dharma debate or dharma combat. Both masters had high realization and flexible minds, and they knew how to turn their minds with the situation. Most people do not know how to respond.

People are generally tied up by the mind's function. In other words, they are rigid and unable to adapt. Zen, however, emphasizes the aliveness and flexibility of the mind, and these qualities are manifested in words and actions. Master Yongjia once said, "Walking is Zen. Sitting is Zen. In speech, silence, movement and stillness, the essence rests at ease." As one reaches this stage, the mind is not tied up by its own function, and the alive and flexible mind essence is unfettered by the phenomena it has created.

The mind of most any sentient being chases after the external environment and relies on that external environment to still its own thinking. As the environment changes, the mind engages in an endless, reactive cycle of changes. For a sage, the environment follows the mind. The sages see phenomena as the results of the mind's function, while ordinary people see phenomena as something concrete in itself. The Mind is pure, and freedom comes from abiding in the Mind essence. If, however, a person's mind rests on phenomena but cannot adapt to changes, it is as if an otherwise healthy person has become accustomed to walking with a cane from the day he learned to walk. If he loses his cane one day, even though he is physically capable of walking he will not know how to do so.

The Mind, in Buddhism, encompasses the mental and material worlds. It is the collective whole of mind-matter non-duality. Zen talked about enlightening the mind and seeing the nature, and in this context the "mind" refers to the phenomena and function of the

Mind and "nature" refers to the essence of all existence. Phenomenon and function are inseparable from the essence. In other words, the mind and nature are inseparable.

Sentient beings often lose awareness when facing phenomena and thus become dependent on them. They let the external environment govern their actions, and the mind loses control. A sentient being creates a world of duality by establishing an external world and an "I" that sees that external world. Because this sense of "I" changes continuously, as does the external world, everything is unstable. However, while the mind seeks refuge in the environment, neither the sense of "I" nor the external environment can remain stable. As the external environment changes, the mind reacts to those changes and the environment again changes along with the new changes in the mind. This generates an endless cycle of reincarnation; a cycle in which there is no peace.

Because all phenomena come from the mind, you should take charge of the phenomena you want to create. Instead of letting the discriminating mind chase after the previous functions of the mind, you can proactively change your mind. The environment will change instantaneously, like the shadow that faithfully follows the individual.

People tend to spend their lives chasing after external phenomena, as if they were chasing their own shadows. They do not realize that phenomena are created by the mind, nor are they aware of where the mind or the phenomena lie. They pollute external phenomena by imposing subjective judgments on phenomena. In fact, the existence of phenomena is objective because it naturally encompasses a certain meaning and value. There is no need to impose additional meaning. No one can see the real world until the subjectivity of the mind is surrendered. Therefore, we must discard the ego attachment in order to transcend the world of duality and enter the state of non-duality. Once we do so, we free ourselves from the cycle of reincarnation.

Zen Master Danxia, after his enlightenment, stayed at Weilin Temple. Once the winter weather grew so cold that he was compelled to cut down some of the wooden Buddha statues and use them as firewood for warmth. The patron of the temple was shocked when he saw this. He leveled harsh criticism against the master and asked angrily, "How could you possibly burn the Buddha statue!?" The master responded calmly, "I wanted to find Buddha relics by burning it." The patron then said, "It is just a piece of wood, how can it have relics inside?" The master continued, "Oh, in that case, let's grab another one for firewood!" The patron's ego attachment was broken down by the Zen master's action, and consequently he attained enlightenment.

Zen teaches that a sentient being does not know his true identity until he is awakened. He does not even know the real person who is talking and eating. Please recite the Buddha's name right now and then ask yourself a question: Is it the mouth that recites the Buddha? Without something else to trigger it, the mouth will not move. Clearly, the mouth cannot recite the Buddha's name. Always keep in mind this question: "Who is the one reciting the Buddha's name?" As we constantly ponder the question in every aspect of life, it will become a prudent weapon, severing all anxiety, delusion and attachment. Use this question as a method to release your ego attachment. At the appropriate moment, an opportunity will allow you to set aside this question and will suddenly reveal the true master within. At that moment, you will see your true face before birth.

The method of engaging the *hua-tou*—the Mind into which thought has not pervaded—is like a great broom that can sweep away every worry, affliction and delusion. If the broom is not removed, eventually it will become the biggest piece of garbage in the room. However, those who do not endeavor to study but instead claim that they do not want to rely on a broom—a spiritual method for purification—will find their lives cluttered with useless garbage. Many Zen practitioners do not firmly understand the principle of cause and effect in spiritual work. Instead, they merely imitate the masters' behavior without abandoning their egos. They will not benefit from the Zen teachings but will only obstruct their spiritual growth.

If the mooring rope is tied to the shore, the boat will go nowhere, regardless of how hard it is rowed. Similarly, when a person is attached to the ego, his speech and behavior are polluted by it. Once the ego is removed, there is a completely refreshed perspective on the world. You must achieve the awakened state in order to gain the attained perspective. When the state of awakening is established, you perceive the essence. There is neither ego nor thought in phenomena, and the reflection of the world is accurate. Only in the state of awakening can the nature of emptiness be known, whereby function and awareness are of emptiness. In the awakened state, mind and matter are one, and essence, form and function are inseparable. There is no duality of subject and object, self and "other" or right and wrong. This moment, the next moment and every moment are in the awakened state.

The essence of Mind is innate and everlasting. Once we remove the delusion that obscures the awakened nature, the awakened state is revealed. Many people feel the need to impose further judgment on top of the innate awareness, but this is superfluous. Whatever the mirror reveals is what is. There is no need to generate another thought to describe it, interpret it and become attached to it.

### Return to the Ultimate Source

The undefiled innate mind, despite being formless, encompasses all there is with clarity. In the Zen classic "Ten Ox Herding Pictures"—a set of images, each accompanied by a short poem in the exploration of a particular Zen doctrine—the eighth image focuses on the teaching of the pure, formless source, in which the inscription states: "Whip, rope, ox and man alike, all belong to emptiness. Vast and infinite the azure sky, no concept of any kind can reach. Over a blazing fire a snowflake cannot survive. In this state at last one comprehends the spirit of the ancient patriarchs."

"Whip, rope, ox and man alike, all belong to emptiness." The subject and object are both emptiness. The spoken word vanishes instantly, just as the mind that can speak also returns to emptiness. Emptiness means the absence of deliberate action: Everything vanishes into emptiness without our interference. "All dharma originates from one source, which is manifested by emptiness." Because everything originates from emptiness, in the moment a sound is heard, the mind that hears the sound and the sound heard by the mind are of emptiness. Even the inward awareness is of emptiness. Once you arrive at the source of life, which is formless and egoless, you arrive at the home of the ancestors.

An enlightened person may recognize the innate awakened state without the complete abandonment of ego. As soon as he or she encounters a certain situation in life, that person's habitual tendencies will take over and the awakened state will be lost. Once this outward tendency is detected and the mind can arouse inward awareness, the original Mind and its awakened state can be reestablished. Thus the thought of inward awareness is like the shepherd's whip. The cause of the inward awareness's arousal is like the shepherd who strikes the ox when it strays. The Mind that gives rise to these thoughts is formless and of emptiness. The function of the Mind is also emptiness. All actualized effects are in vain, creating a state of emptiness as described in the poem.

"Vast and infinite the azure sky, no concept of any kind can reach." The blue sky, although it is wide, does not offer a single place for any matter to rest. Similarly, the formless emptiness is the ultimate source of life, without any abiding. Every Buddha possesses the sign of an imperceptible crown, representing a kind of ultimate monistic wisdom. The formless emptiness of the innate mind, where no concept can reach, is where the essence of creation is present. It is the "crown," or the source of life.

The Mind essence, depending on how it is used, can be contained within a single, insignificant speck of dust or can be so magnificent in its function that it embraces the entire universe at once. We cannot perceive the mind when its functions are withdrawn, and therefore it is said to be hidden in the most insignificant speck of dust. However, when the Mind functions its manifestation can pervade all matter, including that which we cannot see and everything that is seen in the universe. Thus, the Mind can pervade the universe when it is allowed to express its presence.

If the mind can return to the state of original emptiness, its intrinsic awakened nature will not allow any phenomena to find a foothold. No duality can be established. Because not even a single thought can be said to exist in the most original essence of the Mind, all delusions—the judgments that function out of our attachments—are like flakes of snow that immediately dissolve upon contact with a red-hot stove.

The intrinsic awakened nature, when manifested, brings forth peace, tranquility and clarity. In this state, there is no confusion. How can you determine whether your mind is confused? Confusion is manifested through constant interference with the original clarity in the mind due to troubling thoughts, insistences, delusions and paradoxes. The state of innate purity will manifest only in the absence of wandering thoughts and attachments. In such a state, the ultimate foundation of reality is reached, and "at last one comprehends the spirit of the ancient patriarchs." This is the source of life.

Ancient Zen masters practiced by the water and the woods in solitude after their awakening in order to maintain a state of absolute purity. Accordingly, a senior monk, after his enlightenment, went to live in a thatched shed by a river. One day, as he was meditating, he overheard a conversation between two ghosts who were trapped in the water. They said, "Someone with a metal hat will be crossing the river tomorrow. Let's drag him down into the water as our victim!" The next day, the senior monk waited by the river, and there approached a man who had just bought a pot. Because it was raining, he put the pot onto his head, which made it look like a hat. The senior monk told the man, "Lord, with such heavy rain and the water in the river rising, it is dangerous to cross the river. It would be better not to cross today." The man listened to the monk's advice and took a detour.

The monk, in his meditation that night, again heard the two ghosts conversing. "That nosy old monk talked too much. He ruined our plan for reincarnation. Let's go get him!" However, the monk had supernatural powers and immediately withdrew all functioning of the mind to the state of complete emptiness. In other words, he stopped generating any thoughts or functions and reached the state of "vast and infinite the azure sky, no concept of any kind can reach." In that state, no one could locate him, not even Buddha, let alone ghosts or other devilish beings. The two ghosts searched for him but could not find anyone in sight.

Image nine in the "Ten Ox Herding Pictures" represents another level of Zen, which is captioned, "Returned to the Origin, back to the Source; a great effort has been made. As if one has finally become blind and deaf to world concerns. Seated in a hut but hankers not for things outside. Streams meander on of themselves, red flowers naturally bloom red." The phrase "Returned to the Origin, back to the Source," in the first line, refers to finding the ultimate source of life. Indeed, it takes a lot of effort—practicing devotion, recitation, meditation, repentance and prayer—to find the ultimate source of life. All these actions take time and energy, and they often take us down sidetracks and present great trials so that we can eventually find the Way. In that case, as suggested by the second verse, it is better to have ignored the world from the beginning, like the blind and deaf. The mind, instead of acting upon the external world and pursuing worldly matters, can look directly at the source of thoughts and instantly dispel ignorance and attachments.

Afflictions cease to occur when a person accepts the fact that everything is born of the mind. Nirvana, or enlightenment, is therefore the most direct spiritual path. The mind functions every moment. The original Mind's essential nature is always present, so no amount of effort is more effective than the direct abandonment of all thoughts and ego attachments. The Mind manifests the reality. It is not necessary to seek and obtain any other truth than that which is originally there, once we let go of attachments and stop grasping at forms.

The third line of the poem, "Seated in a hut but hankers not for things outside," tells us that we should not discriminate against what is in plain sight. The hut is our own mind. As we refrain from worldly dispositions such as craving, ill will, delusions, paradoxes, spiritual pollutions and attachments until the mind is completely empty and free of ego, we will not impose values or definitions upon matters according to a habitual value system. The water of the river runs without needing anyone to define it as running. The flowers are naturally programmed to bloom regardless of whether anyone values their emergence. When this egoless state of emptiness, awakening and clarity comes forth, everything manifests without the "I." In other words, we see without seeing.

Because a sentient being is filled with habitual tendencies, considerable effort is needed to attain emptiness, awakening and clarity. Habitual tendencies are illusory, and the use of delusion to eliminate delusions is the only way. Zen Master Longya Jiudun illustrated this method of exterminating delusion in a poem: "Zen practice is like starting a fire by drilling into the firewood. Cease not the drilling when the smoke arises. Persist till the sparks appear; then can one return home to the beginning of life." The practice of relinquishing delusions is similar to starting a fire. When the firewood is burning, so is the wooden stick that is used to drill into the firewood. The subject and the object both ultimately vanish, but the key is to persist till the end. Some practitioners may be excited about meditation for a month but then set aside the practice. This is like trying to boil a pot of water. If we turn off the heat halfway through, the warm water will cool. To bring it to a boil, we have to start over. Without consistent practice, the aspiration for the Dao is difficult to firm up and the seated meditation will regress.

Sages have compared practice to the hatching of a chick, because time is required. It will not work if the hen sets upon the egg for a while, leaves and then returns. If we are not engaged in hard work, we will be engaged in something else. It is easy to go astray, but to return to the straight-and-narrow path requires a twofold or even threefold effort. Sometimes, we might not even get another opportunity, time or the ability to return to the Way. Without overcoming the obstacles in this life, the same obstacles will cross our path in the next life. In other words, the same burdens will continue to drag us down from our spiritual progress unless we eliminate them.

Zen Master Shengding Hongyin composed the following poem with inspiration from the one above. "Zen practice is like starting a fire by drilling into firewood. Cease once smoke arises! Wait not till the sparks appear. Or, it will burn you from head to toe." In the first poem, Master Longya is saying that we must not stop studying until we reach our goal. However, Master Shengding Hongyin's analogy is a bit different: He reminds us that, once we reach the top, we should not insist on the path itself anymore. If we insist on our pursuit despite having reached the peak, our persistence will become a hindrance to our understanding. Some people misunderstand the two poems and think that Master Shengding Hongyin disagrees with the earlier master. In fact, the two poems approach the same issue from different angles: They encourage sentient beings to study Zen with balance according to their own strengths and weaknesses.

"Whip, rope, ox and man alike, all belong to emptiness. Vast and infinite the azure sky, no concept of any kind can reach. Over a blazing fire a snowflake cannot survive. In this state at last one comprehends the spirit of the ancient patriarchs." This describes the state of true emptiness, but even here we need to turn the head around. In other words, having reached the source, we are now able to face phenomena without being deceived. We can now function with the pure Mind. This is the next stage: "Returned to the Origin, back to the Source; a great effort has been made. As if one has finally become blind and deaf to world concerns. Seated in a hut but hankers not for things outside. Streams meander on of themselves, red flowers naturally bloom red."

## Believe Firmly in the Innate Mind

A Zen master in the Tang Dynasty, called Master Wuzhu Wenxi, was the lineage-holding student of Master Yangshan. Master Wenxi was from southern China. Once, prior to his attainment of the Way, he visited Mt. Wutai. There the master encountered an old cattle herder at the Vajradhatu cave of Huayen Temple. The old herder invited the master to the temple in which he resided. Once they entered the temple, the herder told a child servant called Junti to take the cattle away, and then he invited the master to sit.

The herder asked Master Wenxi where he was from. The master said, "The south." The old herder continued, "How is the dharma received in the south?" The master said, "In this last dispensation, very few people are willing to put their efforts into spiritual searching." The herder asked, "How many students do you have at the temple in the south?" "About three hundred...maybe five hundred," replied the master.

Master Wenxi asked the old man, "How is the dharma received here?" The old man answered, "The dragon and snakes are intertwined. The saints and the mundane live together." There are many who are reincarnated as saints—whether as monastic or lay persons—but ordinary people cannot perceive their true nature. Furthermore, the innate mind is sacred and empty. It is not of the world. Nevertheless, the effects of the mind are of the world and existence.

Master Wenxi continued: "How many practitioners are there, roughly speaking, in the temples of the north?" The old man answered, "Before, three-three; afterward, three-three." The master did not understand, but the old man offered no explanation. Instead, he changed the subject and asked the master to have some tea. Then, once the herder had taken the teacup in hand he asked, "Do they have this in the south?" The master said they did not. The herder asked, "If not, then what do you use to drink tea?"

The end of the day drew near. Master Wenxi asked if the old man could host him for the night, but the herder refused, claiming that the master still had attachments in the mind. The herder asked the young servant Junti to escort the master out of the temple. The master asked the servant how many was indicated by the statement, "Before, three-three; afterward, three-three." Junti called, "Wenxi," and the master responded. The young servant asked, "How many is it?" Wenxi did not know the answer.

Master Wenxi asked Junti, "Where is this place?" The young servant told him that it was the Vajradhatu cave and Temple Prajna. At last, Master Wenxi realized that the old herder was the manifestation of Manjushri Bodhisattva. So, before he left the place he asked Junti for teaching, and this was what the young servant taught the master: "A face without anger present is the instrument of offering. Words without anger are the fragrance of incense. A mind without anger is a treasure. The state without attachment and defilement is the true permanence."

One who carries no anger on his face and causes no harm with his speech can even bring happiness and enhance others' spiritual practice. While some people, with forked tongues, speak in pleasing languages, they do not bring light to others' lives. Speeches are truly sweet if they bring positive benefits to the world. A mind without anger is the greatest treasure. Both practice and offerings are accomplished with the body, speech and the mind. An unpolluted mind that manifests a peaceful facial expression is the offering, the speech without anger that benefits beings is the true fragrant incense, and the mind without anger is the true treasure.

Junti escorted Master Wenxi out of the temple after he finished his words. When the master turned around to look at the temple right after he stepped out, both the temple and the young man were gone. He saw Manjushri riding upon a lion, traveling through colored clouds. Suddenly, Manjushri vanished into a ragged cloud that had drifted in from the east.

Master Wenxi later attained enlightenment through Master Yangshan's teaching, and consequently he served as the head chef in the kitchen for a period of time. There is a Zen saying that grand masters come from the kitchen. Enlightened masters served in the kitchen because, on one hand, they could learn to form dharma connections with many beings, while on the other hand they could keep, maintain and mature abiding in the essence of the Mind, which brings true joy and wisdom.

One day, as Master Wenxi was cooking, Manjushri's face appeared by the side of the pot. When the master saw it, he hit it with a spatula and said, "Manjushri is Manjushri. Wenxi is Wenxi." What is meant by such a statement? The Mind essence is innate: When you recognize it, there arises confidence because one knows he has control over his own life. Manjushri has his reality, and Wenxi has his own. Once you recognize the innate Mind, there is nothing else upon which you need to rely.

Manjushri then said, "The bitter gourd is connected to a bitter root. A sweet melon is affixed to a candied root. Having practiced over three great eons, I was surprised to be the annoyance of this monk." When perspective is rooted in the innate mind, there will be no distortion, like a mirror reflecting realistic images of all things. Thus the reflection in the mirror is exactly the same as the being who stands before it. In other words, from essence to function it is genuine. The function and the essence are inseparable.

Cultivation requires confidence. You must believe in the innate Mind, and you must recognize that all phenomena are from the innate Mind. Instead of asking others for help, work on yourself to manifest the innate Mind by foregoing attachments. However, before you attain the Way to examine the mind and be at peace with it, you should not take the teachings and heritages of your forefathers lightly. You should not capriciously make up your own way. The unusual behaviors of ancient masters are solely for the purpose of freeing the student's attachments according to his or her readiness and aptitude. They are not things we should superficially imitate.

The ancient wisdom teaches, "Full confidence leads to Buddha-hood." Indeed, the Way is attained when the practitioner attains complete confidence, and true confidence comes from enlighten-ment. The presence of any doubt demonstrates that the mind is not yet firmly established in true understanding. To trust in the teaching of the innate Mind, we must abandon everything. All the paradoxes of charity versus ill will, right versus wrong and ego versus "other" only distort the functioning of the innate mind by subjecting the real-ity to a faulty definition. Only when we dissolve afflictions, attachments and obstructions can the mind of clarity and purity emerge.

First three-three and then three-three,

To recognize the numbers is no trivial feat.

Wenxi spanked the image of Manjushri,

Drawing feet on a snake is quite superfluous.

# 7 THE TRUE MEANING OF ZEN PRACTICE

How pleasing is the beautiful southern scenery by the lake!

Yet, no one cares.

How beautiful are the fireworks at the capital!

 Alas, who inquires?

Emperor Qianlong, who leads an army of carts and ships,

patrolled around town,

showing off his extravagance.

All that trouble in vain because the eyes are covered.

## Life Is a Process of Changes

One must master a principle in order to enter the practice of Zen: The everlasting Mind conceives thoughts at all times. In turn, different thoughts induce their own particular effects and consequences. One day, as Zen Master Baizhang walked in the mountain with his teacher, Zen Master Mazu Daoyi, he saw a flock of wild ducks fly by. Master Mazu asked, "What are those?" "Wild ducks," the student responded. The teacher continued, "Where did the wild ducks go?" Baizhang answered, "They just passed by." Master Mazu Daoyi gave the student's nose a stiff pinch and said, "How could you say they passed by?" The mind is what saw the ducks. It even recognized the ducks. It knew the state of the ducks' passing and the state of the pain in his nose. However, that which knows is not pain, nor is it impermanence. This is a fundamental entry point. One must work on this with diligence.

A sage teaches, "Dissolve past karma as they manifest. Do not create new troubles." We must face our reality without creating further thoughts to complicate the matter, even amid negative circumstances. It was said, "Bodhisattva is concerned about the intentions, while sentient beings only worry about the results." The awakened being knows that results are always consistent with intentions. Therefore, he watches closely for every one of his intentions, even the most insignificant of them. Generally, people are not aware of this subtlety, nor can they manage their thoughts. When negative, habitual tendencies accumulate to a certain extent, afflictions arise. Because most people do not recognize the accumulation of habitual tendencies, they only notice the negative results and become fearful.

Life is doomed to difficulty if we cannot pinpoint our weaknesses through trials. Through self-reflection, however, we can identify our own shortcomings. True Zen practice has no need for clichés; instead, it focuses on mastering the law of cause and effect in our lives. Master Congnian, from Zhaozhou, who was nicknamed "Old Zhaozhou," was enlightened at eighteen years of age. However, at the age of eighty he still traveled widely in order to learn from other monks. He did it for the purpose of tempering his mind so that peace would dwell within him both in motion and stillness.

People, with their various afflictions and attachments, allow their emotions to fluctuate too drastically. There is an old saying: "In a single century, thirty-six thousand days, men are either in stress or suffering illness." True peace is indeed rare. Concerns, attachments, conflicts and ego are all habitual tendencies. However, reflection on the effects of such tendencies and close examination of our state of mind can turn delusion into mindful awareness. Always maintain the awareness and rest at peace. This is the Zen practice.

Many Buddhist organizations today send delegations to visit temples throughout the world. They are merely sightseeing. This is different from the past, when practitioners traveled in order to temper their minds so that they could be at peace wherever they were. Traveling was also a way for them to learn the dharma and other skillful means of practice from accomplished masters. They wanted to go deeper in purifying their minds. True spiritual pilgrimage is for the practitioner to realize his mind, stabilize his mind and purify his mind.

A mind that is tangled will manifest externally through negativity in people, things or events. A person's mind, through its egocentric structure, generates phenomena. Consequently, all that he sees and hears will be consistent with what he should see and hear according to his ego. Each moment people live their lives following this principle, creating a world that is of the ego and for the ego. In other words, through the power of thoughts men organize the energy potential of this universe according to the vibratory resonance of their own thinking patterns and thus create various physical phenomena. Although we believe we see the same thing that someone else sees, it is in fact due to the similarity in your thinking patterns that any two people can fashion the same image in their separate worlds.

The Three Realms are all just Mind. All phenomena are manifestations of consciousness. The Mind and phenomena are inseparable, and everything is a manifestation of the Mind. Each person's mind has the same capability, but each mind has a unique belief system and mode of perception through which an individual creates the corresponding phenomena. If you try to change the external phenomena without changing the fundamental mode of perception in your mind, the result of your effort will be minimal. Compared to the innumerable thoughts that emanate from the mind every day, we are aware of very few of them. If you rely only on the few thoughts you are aware of as the basis for changing your life's reality, how many changes can you expect to actualize?

The mind has the ability to create all things, but it is challenging to have mastery of the mind and maintain inner peace at all times. It is difficult to conquer your enemies, but the biggest enemy in life is your own mind. Most people have endless concerns in life. Their minds are too scattered and confused by delusions. The patriarchs said, "All beings possess the innate light. Yet when they try to see, there is only darkness." All beings have this innate light but their attachments prevent them from seeing it. They simply do not see their thoughts, nor do they see the cause and effects. Neither do they understand why they come across the specific people, things and situations they encounter in life.

Someone once asked me, "How can a child at birth already have negative karma?" Some people say that some children are born ill because God made them so. Others say illness is created by their own minds. Regardless of the cause, no one can deny the fact that the poor babies are sick and need help. In fact, neither of the above explains the reason for sickness in the very young.

The body and mind are energies. The body and mind change continuously, and energies change continuously. No one can bring with him the body or the mind, but attachments and habitual tendencies can be brought along past physical death. Some think that babies are pure and clean, but babies, though newly born, are in fact old beings in their minds. As they reincarnate into another body, they bring with them the seeds of all their past experiences, or the seeds of habitual tendencies. These seeds manifest into various forms under various conditions.

Changes in life are not linear but are multidirectional. For convenience, life is explained as a process of change where karma brought from previous lives are brought to the new life. For every form of living, whether that of a human, a celestial being or an animal, karma is ever-changing. Energies, too, are constant, perpetually evolving and indivisible. People carry their habits and preferences from their past lives over to their new ones, and consequently babies are born into various circumstances. Some are healthy, but others are sick. Some are born into wealth, while others are born into poverty. The conditions into which one is born are all related to the karma from one's past life. Every moment is in fact a new birth; every thought is a rebirth, or a renewal of life.

If your next thought generates illness within, it is simply the cumulative effect of all your negative habits from the past. Most people are not able to liberate themselves from attachments, nor are they able to dissolve the mind's function into emptiness. Too many attachments and insistences perpetually accumulate, creating an endless flow of negative energy. When negative energy reaches a threshold, illness, poor relationships, worries, trials and other adversities will emerge.

A Chinese proverb says, "In the pathetic can one find something loathsome." The truth of this is seen in the law of energy resonance. Phenomena come to pass with certain sets of causes and conditions. An egotistical person only thinks of things that will benefit him. As a result, he fails to see the reality with objectivity and clarity. When he faces a trial, he will not be able to accept it. Instead, his mind will be filled with opinions.

It is impossible to encounter trials that suddenly arise if you have consistently performed well in the past and the present. Positive energies gather with similar energies. In other words, no negative energy can dwell within positive energy. In the Pure Land, one can find buddha, bodhisattvas and saints, but can an ordinary being be anywhere in sight there? Ordinary beings are filled with afflictions and attachments. They are not able to reach the Pure Land simply because they cannot resonate with that energy.

Present fact is the ultimate explanation of reality. If a thief is caught red-handed, what further explanation is needed to convict him? The facts right now are the results of the past. They are also the accomplishments of all your past efforts. If you encounter a negative experience, that experience stands as solid proof of your shortcoming. To make excuses or accuse other people only shows that you have failed to recognize your own issues and have no desire to improve. The wise learn from fundamental principles, but those who are clever and witty can at least learn from trials. The fool suffers from trials till the end but still does not realize the problem in himself. When difficulty is encountered, all he does is blame others.

It is therefore necessary to take a hard look at your mind during a period of difficulty in order to learn and grow. Identify problems from within, and make the necessary improvements. Be at peace with the facts, whether positive or negative. Generate positive, mindful thoughts instead of worrying about what is already fact. Even if you have not become truly wise, you should at least be clever. In the trials of life, you must assess the direction the mind takes as it generates thoughts. Gain awareness of the bias in the mind due to karma and the habitual tendencies from the past. Only by doing so can one cease the afflictions that come from ignorance.

Habitual tendencies can become dominant. If they do, you will not be able to see the truth objectively. You cannot recognize the thoughts your mind generates, nor will you see the consequences that follow. Therefore, afflictions will accumulate in a downward spiral, becoming chronic and more painful. Most people go through life dwelling on their thoughts, whether positive or negative. This is a form of unconscious thinking driven by delusion and the grasping of sensory stimulations. They are like currents in the ocean of life, fluctuating as they disappear into the endless ocean of afflictions. If you do not maintain control through self-reflection, self-assessment and repentance, it is like using the infinite power of your mind to inflict endless torment on yourself.

Saints, with peace and purity of mind, do not function with attachments. Their thoughts are let go as soon as they arise. They maintain the calmness and wisdom of the Mind while embracing all beings with aspiration and compassion. In Buddhism, there are four major bodhisattvas: Arya Avalokiteshvara represents mercy; Manjushri Bodhisattva, wisdom; Ksitigarbha Bodhisattva, ultimate aspiration; and Samantabhadra Bodhisattva, great actions. Together, the saints strive to achieve immeasurable mercy, wisdom, aspiration and actions. Contrastingly, a sentient being does not know how to use the mind because he does not actually recognize it. He is so full of pain and attachments that he cannot find peace in his life. His mind can only beget boundless pain and suffering.

One should examine the phenomena of attachment and pain in order to discover the root cause and return to the source. In Zen practice, one seeks the origin of thoughts. Locate the source of thoughts and then penetrate into it, and enlightenment will follow. Once enlightened, the work is to abide in the source while being vigilant of thoughts in order to break through the habitual tendencies from the past, one after another. This is the true hard work in Zen practice. There is no need to travel thousands of miles to attain the truth.

Those who are overwhelmed and lost in delusions will fall into pain and afflictions once thoughts arise. The external environment is like the wind, and perceptions are like currents in the ocean. When the wind meets the current—when situation meets habitual tendencies—affliction arises. However, as soon as a person sees the emptiness in everything it is no longer necessary to assert or deny anything. Put down every preference so that the light in the mind can shine forth. With the knowledge that all dharma is from the mind, it is no longer necessary to grasp at phenomena. This is the true Zen practice.

The purpose of Zen practice is not to suppress the current of life, making the mind a pond of stagnant water. Thoughts come and go like waves on the surface of the ocean, but sentient beings are attached to certain waves of thoughts. They identify with them, and they rise and fall with them. The enlightened recognize the fact that the true self is the Mind, which is like the ocean: Regardless of the movements of the waves, the Mind will remain constant and boundless in its capacity.

If you do not locate and recognize the ultimate source of life, your mind will become fixated on the individual currents instead of the ocean. Like the currents that arise and submerge, beings continuously engage in death and birth. Reincarnation continues when there is attachment, propelling forward the endless waves of rootless lives. However, by dwelling at peace in the pure Mind one can enjoy freedom regardless of the storms that occur externally. Life becomes boundless, bringing forth immeasurable merits in the state of liberation.

## The Endless Cycle

Zen teaches that one must "take care of the footstep." The foot implies the source of all phenomena. Thoughts arise in a manner similar to one's forward stride. Every step relies on the movement of the foot; every thought emanates from the mind. When in motion, remain aware of that which is motionless. This is tending to the mind itself and the practice of taking care of the footstep. While the walking person appears to be moving, his movements are in fact the effects invoked by the mind. Thus it is not really the body that is moving. Instead, the body is passive and the true agent of action is the mind. The same applies to all relationships and every corresponding cause and effect. The continuous functioning of the mind creates results, including the physical senses of sight, hearing, smell, taste and touch. These become the channel through which the egocentric mind grasps phenomena.

It is essential that we train ourselves to take care of the footstep in order to obtain and maintain peace in the mind. Meditation allows the mind to practice being the master of itself in a quiet environment, whereas traveling study is to abide in peace amid activity. Actually, when the enlightened are walking they focus on the mind's activities but not the legs. The mind is ceaseless and everlasting. Therefore, the assignment of the practitioner is to take care of the mind.

Elder Zhaozhou opened up his monastery at eighty years of age. Whenever there were visitors, the old master would serve tea. The "Zhaozhou tea" became a well-known method of teaching. While anyone can drink tea, the tea becomes different, given the mindset of the individual. In Zen there are also the "Yunmen cookies," which Zen Master Yunmen served to every visitor at his temple. Then there is the "Linji shout." Zen Master Linji would shout at the visitors when they first came through his doors. The shout was meant to chase away the visitor's delusional mind state. These are examples of the specific methods the sages used in the past as methods convenient to the circumstances.

True Zen practice does not require the Zhaozhou tea, Yunmen cookies or the Linji shout. All it requires is that you understand the reality—the cause and effect—of the present moment with inner peace. The purpose of various methods of religious training is to understand the karma of the present, resolve the karma of the present, reshape the karma of the present and attain the fruits of enlightenment.

Mankind assumes the roles of male, female, adult and child in this realm. With persistent practice, however, a sentient being can become a practitioner. Once a practitioner is able to recognize the mind and break through all delusions and attachments, he will become a saint, a Bodhisattva and ultimately a Buddha. This is the evolutionary process of growth in the role of mankind. Buddhahood means the ultimate, complete fulfillment of life. Buddhas dwell in the Pure Land, while men subsist in a world of affliction and defilement. When there is vexation in the mind, the external world becomes defiled. The mind determines the world it creates.

Spiritual cultivation is to start from the reality of the present moment and understand the fault in the way the mind has functioned. This leads to self-reflection and the gradual transformation of our afflictions on our way to the Pure Land. Some question why the phenomena around them do not improve despite the diligence of their practice. This is because they do not truly understand the karma produced from their minds and correct it, and therefore phenomena will not change.

Zen Master Linji was the founding master of a branch in Zen called Linji. Before he was enlightened, he studied for three years in the assembly of Zen Master Huangbo. During that period, he did not ask the master a single question. It is important to ask questions regarding our spiritual practice, but genuine questions only arise from the sincere effort to change and carry out the hard work needed to make the changes. The sages of the past would only ask questions until they had amended their minds and habitual tendencies, whereby they have come to know the real questions within. When such sincere questioning finally emerges through self-introspection, a breakthrough in spiritual practice is near. A genuine question begets an authentic answer, which in turn can solve real problems. Many people go about their practice as if shopping in the mall, asking many superficial questions here and there. If the questions do not come from a genuine place, answers are not essential because, no matter what the answers are, they will bring no benefit.

Elder Luzhou, head monk of Master Huangdu's assembly, one day asked Linji how long he had been a resident of the temple. Linji answered that he been there for three years. The elder Luzhou continued, "Have you ever consulted with the head master?" Linji replied, "No. I don't know what I should ask." The elder encouraged him to ask the head master about the main purpose of Buddhism. Linji then mustered his courage and asked Master Huangbo, "Master, what is the purpose of Buddhism?" However, the master began to strike him with a staff before he could finish the sentence.

Linji, with Elder Luzhou's encouragement, asked the master the same question three times. Each time, he was struck. Each time, no answer was given. Linji was frustrated with his spiritual obstacles and lack of wisdom. He did not understand why he was hit, nor did he understand why no answer was given. Disillusioned, he decided to bid Master Huangdu farewell, pack up and learn from another master. Master Huangbo said, "You should only go learn from Monk Big Fool."

Linji arrived at Monk Big Fool, whereupon the monk asked Linji where he came from. The student answered, "From Master Huangbo." The enlightened are aware that all dharma are inseparable from the Mind, so they know how to answer questions. Whether one is talking or silent, in motion or stillness, everything is the Mind. So, it was impossible for Master Linji to move the changing body and the changing thoughts from Master Huangdu to Monk Big Fool. Only those with self-attachment think they can bring anything with them.

Even though it was then a customary practice to strike a student if he gave an answer that was not in accordance with the enlightened state, Monk Big Fool did not point out the error on the spot. Instead, he asked Linji what he had done at Huangbo's assembly. Linji told him the story of the three strikes he had received from Master Huangbo. He even told the teacher that he did not understand what he had done wrong. The senior monk grabbed his collar angrily after he heard the story and said, "Oh, your compassionate teacher, who was so patient in teaching you! And you come here to ask questions about what you did wrong!?"

Linji was awakened at that moment. He said immediately, "Now I see how little did Master Huangbo teach about! There is nothing much!" Monk Big Fool became even angrier and said, "You bedwetting idiot! You were just asking what you had done wrong. How can you now possibly say this kind of thing about your teacher!?" Linji hit Monk Big Fool three times under the ribs. With his mind directing his actions, the senior monk knew how to respond because he had the mastery of the mind to know how to advance, retreat, hold on or let go. The senior monk pushed the student away and said, "Huangbo is your teacher, this is none of my business."

Linji returned to Master Huangbo. The master saw him and said, "This person keeps going back and forth. When will be the end of this?" Thoughts, bodies and delusions are all travelers in life. Changing at all times, they come and go, eventually return unto dust. The failure to know the mind is like a failure to know the master or host of our lives and instead only chase after illusions that come and go. Most people who have read the above koan fail to notice the significance of these seemingly insignificant words. When Master Huangbo said, "When will this going back and forth end," his question contained an important message.

The process of coming and going is the birth and death of phenomena, like chasing after shadows and sounds. A mind that creates happiness makes a person happy, but a mind that creates vexation makes him worried. In this way men chase and turn with fleeting phenomena, never knowing the source of everything. While going back and forth between different spiritual communities, it is still possible to maintain a certain degree of practice. At least it is much better than many people nowadays, who constantly wander back and forth among worldly conflicts and afflictions.

Linji, following Master Huangbo's remark, reported to him what had happened during his encounter with Monk Big Fool. The master said, "That nosy Big Fool talked too much! I shall beat him up the next time I see him." Linji responded in surprise, "You don't need to wait. You can do your beating right now." With that, he raised his hand and slapped the master on the face.

Why did Master Huangbo hit Linji three times when the student asked him the meaning of Buddhism? If you were to ask me the purpose of Buddhism now, my mind would function in such a way as to hit you. At the same time, your mind would function to take up such hitting as a consequence. Therefore, the action of hitting is already the answer to you. It is the answer right in front of you. Buddhism is about causality, in which the mind is the cause and the function and forms are the effects. The mind creates phenomena every moment, and hitting is merely a phenomenon. Phenomena occur at the moment the mind functions. This is the doctrine that the young master Linji realized from this experience. So, wait not, for now is now. Now is not the past, the present or the future. The cause, as it is now, produces the result now.

The highest principle in Buddhism is to manifest the reality in each moment. The Mind's function resonates with the infinite, boundless causes and conditions to become the reality of this moment. The corresponding results are produced at the precise moment of the Mind's functioning. Causes and results are simultaneous; Mind and Buddha are inseparable. The Mind functions through the infinite, boundless connections of mutually penetrating realms, and the Mind manifests this moment's causality and results. This principle is the law behind the creation of phenomena.

Life's events, whether favorable or adverse, are the actualization of reality when various factors and conditions came together; that is, when the prerequisites for the underlying principle have been satisfied. Principle provides the explanation for the origin and destination of the present moment's phenomena. Therefore, we cannot understand the nature of the mind or causality. We cannot understand the relationship between the manifestation and the principles, or the conditional and dependent origination of various phenomena in life. This is your life, and it is up to you to improve and elevate it. The practice is to take care of your own mind. No benefit will result simply because a person can grasp an abundance of knowledge.

An ancient poem goes like this: "By the end of the winter in April, while most plants struggle to survive, cherry blossoms by the temple are prospering beautifully. As the man in the garden longs anxiously for signs of spring, the springtide has already stolen in quietly." Thoughts, like flowers, vanish as soon as they flourish; while the mind's function is long gone, the mind is ever-present. Depending on how one uses the mind, it manifests continuously in life. It can create anger at one moment and happiness in the next. It can induce hardship in the previous moment but favorable circumstances in the present. The cherry blossoms by the temple still bloom, because they do not drift with changes.

One cannot blindly chase the seasons of life in the hope of a renewed life. Instead, try to gain awareness that the Mind is the creator of seasons. As you rediscover the innate mind, liberation will become an eternal companion, there within you at every moment and every turn in life. A pure mind flourishes, constantly bringing new life to the world, so there is no need to be concerned about the cycle of life and death in the physical world. Do not surrender to fluctuating phenomena. Every current originates from the mind and is therefore dependent upon the mind. Understand the nature of the mind, the law of causality, the relationship between the principle and manifestations, and the conditional and dependent origination of phenomena of this present moment's reality. This is the beginning of the practice. A sectarian view of Zen, Christianity or any scriptural religion will not reveal the Way to you. You must instead seek diligently from the Mind. You must focus your practice on the Mind and manifest from the pure characteristic of the Mind in order to establish a solid foundation for spiritual growth.

> Look not at the clichés like "Zhaozhou Tea" that are
> flooding the world.
> The wise find truth inward, like locating the intestine
>  only in the body.
> Revolve among afflictions for the season,
> only to find that autumn has already scattered the leaves
> in front of the cypress.

# 8 THE CHANGEOVER

While the peonies at the palace show off their beauty,

the osmanthus emit fragrance throughout August.

White spruce flowers sprinkle little snowy stars

across the summer field.

A boat rests hidden among vast aloe blossoms.

## To Understand Life Is to Master the Dharma

The enlightened one becomes the master of his or her life, the present and the future. Enlightenment means a person can discern the innate mind. Prior to enlightenment, the sentient being fills his mind with duality, leaving no room for the dharma and its eternal purity. Enlightenment comes when we know where the mind abides, how it initiates effects and what the corresponding results are. The mind is awakened only when we are able to locate the source of life. Contrastingly, those who have not awakened are unaware of the mind's activity and its effects. They have no immediate understanding of the relationship between the causes and their consequences. As a result, they are compelled to wrestle with numerous afflictions and attachments.

Most people misinterpret the dharma as the study of Buddhist scriptures, but such a definition is certainly too narrow. The mind's function is the dharma. Unfortunately, without a sense of the mind's activity the dharma taught by the Buddha is reduced to the mundane understanding of sentient beings. The dharma exists between our breaths and even among the specks of dust. It exists in every action throughout our day-to-day lives. Every thought that emanates from the mind is the dharma. Overwhelmed with delusions, mankind finds himself weighed down with the physical life, without the time needed for self-reflection. Subsequently, the mind, despite its original purity, is corrupted. When the sentient being does not know where the mind is and how it functions, ego, paradoxes, torments and adversities will cause endless trouble. The dharma therefore emphasizes that we should follow the precepts as the means to gain steadfastness and wisdom.

The purpose of the scriptures is to teach people the correct value system so that they can identify their problems and choose to forsake them. There is no need to analyze the scriptures. Prior to enlightenment, the sentient being, filled with attachments, will not truly comprehend the scriptures. We are incapable of comprehending any concept beyond our attachments unless we can break the barricade to spirituality.

The word "Buddha" means pure nature. This pureness in the mind comes from enlightenment. The word "dharma" means phenomena or effects, which include all the phenomena evoked by a pure mind. The dharma can include such rudimentary activities as going to the bathroom, sweeping the floor or eating, as well as meditating and chanting, as long as the mind is pure. When the mind is impure, everything from it is polluted. Consequently, we must focus on the attainment of a pure mind in order to attain the true dharma.

Paradoxes, such as good and evil, right and wrong, and ego versus "other," are all brought forth by men. Life is a continuous series of consequences. It is unnecessary to seek answers about life from others. Instead, we need only rely on introspection: "Why did I think that way? Why did I see it that way? Why did I do it that way?" Life, as the creation of the Mind, is an aggregated phenomenon of the Mind, which is the source of life. The direction we take in life depends on the direction in which the mind is engaged. In other words, destiny is in the hands of the individual.

A man has a destiny as a man, and a woman has a destiny as a woman. A serious outlook results in a staid life, while an ugly appearance belies a loathsome existence. One who is filled with happiness always encounters happiness, whereas the one who is worrisome will be doomed to affliction. Our fates are not predetermined by the Buddha or our parents. Instead, each person's fate is actualized within his mind.

As a person becomes more familiar with his own existence, his comprehension of the dharma increases. Mahayana Buddhism teaches charity, the observance of Buddhist precepts, endurance, energetic effort, meditation and wisdom. These values are taught because mankind is fraught with so many issues. By following these spiritual methods, we can gain the ability to resolve the issues. Thus we have the saying, "To cure all minds, Buddha teaches all dharma. Without any mind, there is no use for any dharma."

Ask yourself a question: Have you ever performed charitable acts? Even if you have, you might have done so only rarely, and you might have even experienced inner conflict or vexation due to your charitable behavior. Life is ever-evolving, and consequently nothing remains unchanged. Youth does not linger, nor do money and relationships. Ironically, in the process of accumulating these impermanent possessions, afflictions grow. It is easiest for mankind to relinquish his time, but it is the most confounding thing for him to give up his worries. From birth to death, many changes take place. In theory, one's worries should come and go like everything else, but unfortunately they do not. For most people, the primary accumulation of life experience is not wisdom but worry.

People are easily attached to habits, and they become firmly dedicated to numerous assumptions. This behavior of attachment defies the law of impermanence. Confucianism teaches that men must conform to nature instead of attempting to resist its unceasing law. Afflictions come when a person's thinking and behavior violate the Universal Truth. There is just one reason for our afflictions: the violation of the Universal Truth as it exists in the Mind. Afflictions are a manifestation of our deviation from the truth. To narrow the distance from the truth, we must learn of the truth, practice the truth and utilize the truth through spiritual practice.

## Find a Way to Life Through Persistent Practice of the Truth

Master Huairang, of Nanyue, once traveled to Mt. Songshan to visit Master Hui'an. He was accompanied by his fellow practitioner, Monk Tan Ran. Master Hui'an is generally known as the "royal teacher," because he had been the emperor's teacher. The two visiting monks asked the royal teacher, "What was the purpose of Buddha's visit to the West?" The royal teacher asked in reply, "Why don't you ask yourself why you came here?" They asked,

"So, why are we here?" The royal teacher answered, "You should look inward to the subtle functions within." They continued and asked, "What are the subtle functions within us?" The senior master opened his eyes briefly and closed them again. The opening and closing of the eyes is the delicate function. When understood, this function becomes the dharma as well as the reason for Buddha's visit to the West. Monk Tan Ran was awakened at the moment he saw what the royal teacher had done, but Master Huairang still did not realize the meaning behind it. In Buddhist philosophy, the timing for him to understand the precept had not yet matured. So, he went to visit the Sixth Patriarch, Master Huineng.

Patriarch Huineng asked Master Huairang, "Where did you come from?" He replied, "Mt. Songshan." The patriarch then asked, "What cometh and how?" What can one derive from this question? Thoughts, bodies and energies evolve momentarily. It is impossible to carry the changes from one moment into the next. The phenomena that occur in a single moment can belong only to that particular moment. This is what the patriarch was teaching with his question.

Master Huairang of Mt. Songshan was not the same as Master Huairang right at the moment he answered the Sixth Patriarch's question. In fact, Master Huairang of Mt. Songshan had ceased to exist. Consider another example: An average person might say, "I'm going to the market." In fact, it is a function from the pure emptiness of the Mind that establishes the phenomenon of the person being at the market. Most people will connect various phenomena with ego into a linear series of changes, whereupon they incorrectly conclude that they are going to the market.

The common fixation with phenomena is caused by the continuous habitual tendency of the ego to seize external phenomena. The perception of "I" is, for most people, an illusion resulting from that same outward tendency to grasp at the external. This pressure leads people to assume that they do not change as they travel from one location to another.

Patriarch Huineng asked Master Huairang, "What cometh and how," but the student could not answer. Some readers of the scripture may boast that they have the answer to this question. However, if their spirituality has not reached the appropriate level, their answer is only delusional. It is not sincere understanding. True understanding comes when you can utilize the knowledge as freely as you can manipulate your hand. Your teacher's mastery in precepts belongs to him. The records in the scriptures are Buddha's knowledge. If you think you comprehend the teachings simply because you can mimic the words, it is the same as grabbing onto your teacher's or Buddha's hand and asking, "Why can't I move my hands?"

Pay attention if you preach to others the precepts from your teacher, which you presume to have mastered even though you have not practiced them. This behavior indicates your ignorance and the inability to practice self-reflection. If your teacher asks you, "What cometh? Why cometh?" you may come up with many answers. You may say, "I've read this koan," or you may say, "I understand this one." You might even answer, "It is due to the existence of impermanence," or, "It is because a living mind is active every moment." Regardless of how clever your answers may sound, if your actions and spirituality do not catch up to the level of your answer, your ego merely pretends to have the understanding.

People often assume they understand, but such understanding is merely a fabrication. Therefore, you must exercise self-reflection often. Always bear in mind the question, "What do I really know?" It is true knowledge to hold what you know and admit what you do not. Fake understanding is the most harmful poison in the world. To progress, you must humble yourself and learn with diligence.

## There Is No Excuse

It is a great concern, when teaching students, that they tend to say "but." For example, I might tell them to work hard, be serious in their study and engage in self-reflection. Often a student will respond by saying, "Yes, I know, but…." The use of the word "but" indicates that the student is taking a detour, retreating from his study or opting for a longer route than is necessary. To put it plainly, "but" signifies an excuse. If the student says, "Teacher, you are right, but…," he is telling me that he is choosing a different route than what I am teaching.

The seemingly insignificant word "but" has a particular significance in life. Each time a person uses the word "but," he is making a choice on the path he takes. I often tell my students that whenever they use the word "but" they are telling me that even though I am teaching them the Way, they decide not to follow. How can I possibly teach students who regularly give me excuses by using "but"? I have no choice. I can only let them go. Letting them go means I can only tell them this: "Why don't you think about a better way to handle it?" That way, they are allowed to go straight to the dead end of their choice. The student who relies on the use of "but" will enter the path of death and darkness, not the path of light and life.

Someone once asked Old Zhaozhou, "As such an accomplished master, you must be very compassionate. Then, why do rabbits always run away from you?" The senior monk answered straightforwardly, "I love to kill." If I correct my students each time they use the word "but," I become the killer of their spiritual denial. However, if I let them go I simply leave them to fend for themselves. Excuses are not helpful to them. In fact, it is exactly because of the many occasions in the past, when they have used "but" and "because," that they have reached their present circumstances. If they continue to follow their excuses, they will eventually come to a spiritual dead end.

These students are in their present state because of the various uncontrollable limitations in their lives. They grab onto these restraints and continue to say "but": "But I don't have time to work hard." "But I have a lot to do." "But I think that I should take it slow on this." This indicates that they are following a path created by the same conditions that have brought difficulties to them. They are sure to reach a dead end.

The person who constantly gives excuses has a rigid life. His troubles remain because he lacks the courage or the ability to overcome problems. What is the fundamental reason for a person's refusal of the truth? It is rooted in the inability to conduct self-reflection. The individual overestimates his spirituality; he assumes disproportionate intelligence and power. His ignorance drives him even further from enlightenment. Due to the absence of steadfastness, he misjudges his place on the path of spiritual destiny.

One's level of spirituality can be assessed in the following way: First, observe whether your mind can direct your thoughts while meditating. Secondly, pay attention in your daily life to see whether you hold onto any worries. If the mind can direct your thoughts during a meditation session and you have no worry in life, it reveals that you truly understand the Buddhist precepts. Zen masters said, "I do not have a lot of idle furniture here. That furniture is just for showing off. It does not present any actual functionality." Many Buddhists are very familiar with Buddhist doctrines. They speak of the Three Vehicles of Learning, the Six Paramitas, the exoteric and the esoteric, and many more, as if they know everything. However, in the end they remain stuck in their afflictions. One cannot wash the hands clean just by fully opening the tap.

The mind is neither good nor evil. We must delve into the mind to find the place where neither concept exists. If a person's mind chases after any cause, whether charitable or evil, solely because of the impermanent thought at the moment he is simply following his thoughts blindly. Let us consider the example of a student who says "but" by comparison to Master Linji's parable of the currents and the ocean: Suppose that I tell such a student, "You have too many worries and are too attached to the physical world. You should be more focused in your practice and reflect on yourself more often." Next, suppose that the student responds by saying, "Teacher, I have already tried my best, but I am still not progressing." If I tell him to continue what he is doing, I allow him to drift with the currents of the ocean. In this case, I am cruelly watching him fall into the deep end of the pool of spiritual death. On the other hand, I reclaim the situation if I confront him by saying, "Nonsense! You need to practice more self-reflection. You lack spiritual focus and wisdom but are filled with ignorance and delusions." These are my instructions for a spiritual makeover, but few would accept such criticism.

Master Huairang, of Nanyue, could not answer Patriarch Huineng's question. In Zen, to know something means you have actualized it as the reality. There is nothing blurry between the knowing and the not knowing. If one stuffs a concept that he does not understand into his mind, won't it ineffectively occupy space in the mind? An old adage presents this idea in a wise and vivid way: "Plowing through scriptures without understanding them is like a person who sees much but appreciates less than the blind. Buddhist scriptures take up vast space in one's mind. However, without the willingness to till his mind, weeds grew everywhere. Where can the grain grow?"

Thus, Master Huairang decided to dwell with Patriarch Huineng. He studied under the patriarch for eight years prior to his enlightenment. One day, after he was enlightened, he went to the teacher in regard to something he had learned. He said, "To say it is like something misses the point." As the Mind illustrates different functions, the corresponding phenomena will be different. The Mind is not within anything, nor is the Mind outside anything. Neither is it in the middle of anywhere. The Mind is beyond all there is, but it can create all. This is why the Mind does not resemble anything.

Patriarch Huineng responded to Master Huairang with the question, "Then, do you still need to practice?" The student answered, "Emptiness cannot be cultivated; it is lost due to defilement." So, we still need to practice, but the practice is that of remaining free of defilement. A clean mind is one that is free of delusions due to worries, attachments or paradoxes of the external world. It focuses on the pureness within. The constancy of pureness in the mind requires diligent practice. Anyone—even the unenlightened—can engage in this spiritual practice. The key to such practice is to persist in self-reflection. Always remember this principle: If you have any worry or cannot gain a sense of peace in the mind, there must be something wrong within. Any excuse would only lead to samsara and reincarnation. For example, someone says, "Even though I have lost a lot of money, still, I have worked very hard." As nice as the comment might sound, it has no practical meaning.

You have not truly practiced self-reflection until you discover the falseness within. If you use a problematic mind to try to find weaknesses within, you are bound to fail. Even if you do detect weaknesses, such a discovery will be in error. How can you determine whether you have truly found weakness through self-reflection? After rigorous self-examination and corresponding hard work, if you still have many worries and afflictions, such self-examinations are not really genuine because the problem remains. If you are not skilled in self-reflection you will have no chance of being enlightened, because enlightenment is achieved by breaking your attachment. After all, it is your own mind. Both confusion and enlightenment can occur through your own doing.

Patriarch Huineng thus replied to Master Huairang: "Just this undefiled purity is exactly the one thing that Buddha treasures. So do you, and so do I." This is affirming the Mind with the Mind: You know it, and the master knows it. This is the essence of what Buddha mastered. It is the same for all Buddhas and saints of the past. Thoughts, effects and phenomena are all induced by the mind and manifested from the mind. Buddhist practice requires that we see things through the pureness of the mind but not from its delusions. The so-called pureness is the innate form of the mind. It transcends all paradoxes of filth and purity, saints and sentient beings, right and wrong, and ego versus others.

The Second Patriarch Huike, upon his first encounter with Bodhidharma, said, "My mind does not feel peace." Bodhidharma responded and said, "Give me thy mind and I shall give it peace." If I were to tell you the same thing after you complain to me about your troubles, there would certainly be a lot to pull out from your mind. However, in Huike's candid effort to observe the mind he discovered that he "looked but could not find it."

A Buddhist practitioner must be sincere in her desire to seek freedom from life or death, to seek truth and to seek the correct path. Once, during a session, a fellow student admired my sitting posture and asked me quietly, "How did you learn to sit so well? Can you teach me?" I told him, "When you stick the phrase 'life and death' onto your forehead, you will find the answer to the question."

Spiritual practice is for the purpose of transforming and enhancing the quality of our lives, and finding the correct way, or the

right from WRong
over good vs. evil

we know
whats right
and wrong
we are taught
good
&
evil

Way toward the light. Buddha is, in fact, the pure mind. Functions from the innate mind are the dharma. This is the simple precept that thousands of scriptures are trying to teach. So, isn't it more direct and natural for you to search the mind instead of searching the scriptures?

Master Xuefeng once studied and traveled with his fellow disciple, Monk Yantou. They encountered a snowstorm on the way and were unable to move forward. Master Xuefeng was very diligent. He meditated each day. Contrastingly, Monk Yantou spent most of his time sleeping. One day, Master Xuefeng could not help his frustration and criticized his fellow disciple: "We are on a quest to learn, but you have not done much more than sleeping." Monk Yantou said, "Look at you. You meditate every day, sitting there like the earth-god statue in the village." Monk Xuefeng said, "It is because I do not feel peace in my mind." Monk Yantou, being enlightened, said, "Tell me all of your disturbing thoughts, one by one. If they are on the right path, I will help you confirm them. If not, I will ask you to disregard them."

The practice of Buddhism involves carrying on the right and foregoing the wrong. Huike concluded that he "looked but could not find the mind" after he searched diligently step by step. He explored inward and peeled off his ego, layer by layer. When he reached the ultimate end to the innate mind, he found that the mind had no physical presence. Thus the answer came from his spiritual experience, not through knowledge obtained from a text. He truly felt the presence of the ultimately pure innate mind in his own experience. An average person may give a similar answer to the same question, saying, "The mind has no physical presence, so I cannot find it." However, such an answer is logical knowledge obtained from text; it is not an enlightened understanding gained through self-reflection.

Master Mazu Daoyi came down with an illness. Someone came to visit him and asked, "Master, how have you been lately?" Mazu Daoyi replied, "I am able to face Buddha day and night." Some understand this koan as his ability to master the mind by day and by night, but such an understanding is shallow. Others assume the teaching to be that the mind could initiate all effects, whether good or evil, and that all phenomena are rooted in the mind. This, however, does not fit the koan. Neither interpretation captures the meaning of the story. This koan appears to be simple, but actually it presents a very deep meaning. Zen masters said, "To attain the Way, one must be observant of the subtleties."

Those who are enlightened use koans to test the depth of their realization, but teachers use them to test students' level of enlightenment. Be particularly cautious when you think you have mastered a teaching. If you pretend to know but actually do not, it will only tarnish your spiritual virtue. The meditation hall is a sacred place for self-improvement. In the meditation hall, you should remain quiet unless you have genuine realizations to share. To attain the dharma, you must begin your practice from the foundation of the four postures. The four postures are symbolic of the ways in which we can examine ourselves inwardly. Those who have not awakened are not disciplined in their postures. They must diminish their ego, opinion, pride and anger to the extent that only the goodness remains and the spiritual weakness vanishes.

It is certainly challenging to face oneself and let go of oneself. However, it is essential that we do so. In order to see the innate mind and its purity, you must forego all that is ignorant and unclean. Be patient and persistent. It might be difficult at first, but it will get better. Sentient beings are so obsessed with their worries and attachments that they do not even realize it when these worries and attachments become habitual. Their lives are filled with familiar concerns and material attachments. They must exercise their spirituality because they have not familiarized themselves with awareness of their own thoughts, meditation and self-reflection.

## Habitual Tendencies Come from Your Own Brainwashing

Actions have their basis in thoughts, and different ideas lead to different behaviors. Therefore, as you alter your thoughts your actions will change. To amend thoughts, we must pay attention to the mind's activity. When the mind continually creates the same stream of thoughts, the stream will evolve into our value system. It will become the default channel for all thoughts. Externally, it manifests in the form of habits. Habitual tendencies are repetitive functions and trends from the mind. Our appearance is a habitual tendency, as are the thoughts and actions to which we are accustomed.

Buddhist practice is intended to cultivate the mind. People often doubt how a practitioner can accomplish such a goal when the mind has no physical presence. In fact, we cultivate the mind by cultivating our way of thinking. Everyone has his own value system.

This value system creates various tastes and colors in life, just as the furniture and decorations create a personalized atmosphere in a home. When the mind is disturbed by afflictions and worries, it signifies that the causality of the mind has deviated from the pureness. This causality must be examined and reconstructed. If you often trip over the clutter in your house, you should rearrange your furnishings and remove anything that poses an obstruction. This principle also applies to clearing up the mind.

One must be willing to amend his or her ways when an obstacle is encountered. There is a Chinese saying: "When the mountain stands in one's way, the road can be altered. When the road cannot be altered, the traveler must change himself." Change comes with the adjustment of the mind. The presence of worry, anger, anxiety and other negative thoughts indicates that the mind has reached the point at which something stands in the way and hinders further progress. Without opening the mind, you will not be able to break through the obstacles. Instead, you will be strangled by afflictions. Ignorant is the person who does not recognize the need for correction of the mind in order to cease afflictions. Transformation can only come about by identifying habitual tendencies through close observation of the habitual tendencies beneath the dissatisfaction of a given situation.

Three feet of ice cannot form in a single cold day. Similarly, the transformation of habitual tendencies cannot occur so quickly. We must first observe these tendencies in order to understand them and transform them. Human beings live with many habits. As we talk, eat, walk and drive, we observe our surroundings. We are constantly controlled by our habits. Habitual tendencies prevent the mind from calming down when we meditate. Even though we use various methods—such as breath counting and engaging hua-tou—to help bring the mind to pureness, we are astonished to find that the mind remains full of scattered thoughts. These thoughts are all delusive manifestations of habitual tendencies.

The uncontrollable, emotional fluctuations in our daily lives are even more significant delusions. Is it possible to ignore them? That is more easily said than done. The reasons for the failure to transform habitual tendencies include a lack of ability for self-reflection, a lack of steadfastness in the mind, a lack of understanding in regard to the dharma and a lack of practice in real life. It takes a long time to create and develop a habitual tendency, and habitual tendencies are persistent in their growth. When habitual tendencies overpower the control of the mind, spiritual growth will stagnate.

One must use the right method of practice to develop stead-fastness in order to gradually transform attachments in the mind and conquer habitual tendencies. Otherwise, regardless of the effort in practice and the type of practice you use, your spiritual practice will be a mere formality. You can monitor spiritual prog-ress by observing your daily interactions with people and affairs, afflictions and habitual tendencies, as well as by observing the level of peace in the mind. Many practice Buddhism as if they are jog-ging in place. They work at it, and they sweat over it. Ultimately, they fail to move beyond the starting point. Some seem to practice devotedly for a few years without seeing any progress, because they have failed to see their own problems. They fail to transform their deep-rooted attachments and habitual tendencies.

Habitual tendencies are formed subtly. For example, you might not be interested in politics at the beginning, but by pure chance you hear a politician's speech and agree with what he has said. You remember the various points he has made. Gradually, your innate mind creates corresponding thoughts, one after another. Once the habit of agreeing is formed, you cannot help but affirm the stance of that person's political party. The change is very inconspicuous. Therefore, you must pay close attention to the pattern of causality in order to identify the change.

The empty Mind is like a dense forest, so vast that you cannot see the edge. At first, there is no trail in the forest. Believing in a concept is like cutting down a tree to open up a space. The felling of a tree allows one to see the potential for a trail, so one will cut down more trees in the same direction in order to create the trail. Once the trail is formed, it naturally becomes the only way out of the forest. In other words, when people convince themselves what is right or wrong in certain things, they unconsciously brainwash themselves and reinforce their presumptions.

The empty Mind creates a thought, whereupon the phenomenon is manifested. This in turn induces a feeling, which strengthens the momentum that drives the creation of similar thoughts. Thus the stronger momentum and thought will create more phenomena of the same kind. Habitual tendencies are self-prompted and fostered in this manner. As people gradually develop the characteristics in their thinking and personalities, their value systems result from self-inflicted brainwashing. To gain an objective understanding of the world, solve problems and transform yourself, you must forsake this paradoxical belief system of right or wrong and ego versus "other." You must be able to analyze reality as it is, because the insistence in your belief will prevent you from seeing the root of your opinions.

Humans are easily confused. They are at a loss as to why they are where they are today. Despite mankind's proud possession of rationality, such rationality is limited. There are many pitfalls in human rationality, and they are due to self-interpretation. These pitfalls prevent people from discussing events in an objective way. Sakyamuni Buddha once said, "If everyone thinks that his own view is right, there will be no truth in the world."

The confused mind has lost sight of the nature of the Mind. It is like a person lost in the forest, urgently seeking a way out. He forces his way forward mechanically in an unknown direction, cutting down all the trees in his way. To fundamentally solve problems in life, we must examine our own thoughts and personalities. Stop chopping down trees randomly. Stand still instead, and ask yourself, "Why do I cut down these trees?" The only way out is to understand why you cut down trees in that certain direction. Otherwise, you will continue to chop down trees with a brainwashed mind.

## There Is No Coincidence

The circumstances of life are inevitable, not coincidental. The route determines the scenery, and our frame of mind determines our reality. A happy mind brings forth laughter, whereas sad thoughts induce tears. A quarrelsome person will naturally find himself in situations that lead to arguments. A Chinese idiom says, "People who get killed in fights are the ones who know how to fight.

People who are drowned are the ones who know how to swim." The people, events and worries we encounter are the inevitable phenomena created by our personalities and habitual tendencies.

A path seems to open up when we chop down trees in one direction amid an immeasurably vast forest. How can one ensure that the chosen direction will lead to an exit? It is not the right solution to fell trees randomly. We must first elevate ourselves high enough to obtain a bird's-eye view of the entire forest. Therefore, the solution lies in transcendence, which calls for the elevation of our present lives.

The thoughts generated in the mind tend to impose interpretations onto what we encounter. If interpreted accurately, the issues will be resolved. Unfortunately, human beings rarely see things rationally and objectively, so they are unable to change their predicaments. Habitual tendencies are trails formed over time by blindly felling trees in the forest of the mind.

Obliviousness to the truth will only bring forth a self-induced suffering, which in Buddhism is called negative karma. A more positive outlook interprets them as life lessons. If a person constantly brainwashes himself, using a fixated frame of logic to justify his predicament, he will find no way to distinguish truth from what he perceives to be true.

If you trip over a particular spot each time you encounter it, why not remove the object that trips you? Most people are unwilling to accept lessons in life. Only the wise will explore them deeply by asking, "Why do I come across this lesson?" After self-examination, the wise person will eventually realize that the mind produces certain effects according to habitual tendencies, which bring forth the corresponding reality.

Phenomena are produced out of the molds of habitual tendencies. These tendencies create thoughts and experiences, one after another, until they form a special logical system in the mind. Once such a system is built, a person's frame of mind is set in stone. The only logical explanation for why he has a particular opinion at a particular moment is: "I am used to thinking this way." There is no doubt that a man who has just crawled out of a manure pit stinks. Human minds are filled with evil, troubling thoughts, which make a manure pit of the mind. When we crawl out of such a mind, we will certainly stink too. The actual manifestations of this are that we will be aggressive in our speech and will have conflictive, worrisome thoughts.

The definition of facts based on habitual tendencies splits the world into binary oppositions, where different emotions flourish. A person easily gets upset and anxious in response to his own opinion. As it takes time and energy to resolve emotional issues, he loses opportunities to seek the truth and correct his mistakes. It would be much more efficient to use his time and energy to focus on resolving the actual problems that produced the emotion instead of dealing with the emotional. For example, someone spots some litter on the floor and starts to discuss what kind of litter it is, where it came from and who should remove it. In fact, he could have simply taken a broom in hand and swept up the litter. The problem would be resolved in no time.

I will give you another example: When juice is accidentally spilled on someone by another, generally his immediate reaction would be to feel annoyed. So, instead of dealing with the soiled shirt he allows himself to be carried away with emotions. It is initially a very simple matter to clean or change the shirt. However, many people, by allowing themselves to be carried away with emotions caused by habitual tendencies, complicate an already problematic situation. If one can simply let go of the emotions and directly solve problems, life will be much more efficient and liberating.

Life is a play that we write, direct and perform by ourselves. There is no need to ask why we encounter certain people or events, because they are already factual. It is important to understand ourselves and know the level of our ignorance and worries. Generally speaking, when a person encounters injustice in life his habitual tendencies and worries will increase in the process of resolving the issue. He encourages the habitual tendencies by constantly creating and defining phenomena through the same tendencies. As a result, emotional fluctuations arise. These emotions cause pain and affliction in the mind.

Many people unconsciously deepen their attachments every moment of their lives, doing so to such an extent that they cannot be further away from the truth and solutions to their problems. People often say, "I did not know it would turn out this way." Presumptions produce unexpected results, and too many presumptions will cause problems for oneself and others. Therefore, presumptions are the most dangerous traps in life. They lay down the path by which a person will ultimately dig his own grave.

Unconscious thoughts lead to senseless actions. When you think about how many thoughts you actually observe in a day, you will realize the incredible depth and expanse of unconscious thoughts you have on a regular basis. Subsequently, changes in life become limited. If people cannot even handle all the problems that sprout from phenomena, how can they possibly find time to realize their innate minds? Problems occur when people impose definitions onto facts, thus disturbing the peace in the mind. Therefore, we must avoid such definitions. A disturbed mind is distant from purity, the saints, the practice of the truth and the true understanding of reality.

Consider the example of a student who was engaged in breath-counting as a means to calm the mind for meditation. He was thinking about the number "one," but the number did not appear in his mind. Instead, he was beset by delusions, lethargy and drowsiness. This indicated that he was too far from "home." There was no way for him to perceive a way out or identify a direction. When a person experiences such a difficulty in staying with a single thought in a controlled environment, he will perceive the dominant power of his habitual tendencies. What is worse is that this power governs us most of the time in life. To eliminate habitual tendencies, we must first start with the more obvious ones and then proceed to the subtle ones. When we can reach such a state that we notice thoughts in the mind when we are awake, it will be possible to observe thoughts during sleep. Similarly, if we can notice thoughts when we are not busy, we may be able to observe our thoughts even when we are busy.

Uncontrollable delusions are like water springing from a well. Despite great effort to scoop out the water, the well continues to overflow. What is the balance a practitioner should strive for, as illustrated by this parable? Consider the breath-counting meditation.

When one counts "one…two…three…four," every number should be clearly impressed in the mind without any delusions. This balance means that the amount of water scooped away equals the amount of excess water, so the water no longer overflows. However, the source of the spill remains unknown and the water continues to flow. In other words, the habitual tendencies in the mind continue to induce phenomena. Consequently, a balance that is maintained by scooping out the "water" is merely intended to contain the delusions to a certain degree. Therefore, one is still some distance from the ultimate goal.

A sentient being tends to shape his mind into a particular mode, and he forces life to proceed according to this mode. Anything that departs from this mode makes him feel ill-prepared. Because everything a person faces in life is created by his or her own thoughts and actions, a certain mode will only bring a certain result. From east to west, from the old days till the modern age, humans have not escaped the following pattern: First, a person generates a thought. Once he gets used to this thought, he perpetuates it through use. Eventually, this attachment to habitual tendencies and their perpetuation will bring adversity.

We cannot understand ourselves clearly and objectively without abandoning delusions. Only those who engage in self-reflection find ways to strive on the path of progress. Humans are used to looking outward, but from now on we should examine inwardly, seeking the mind. Disregard the external environment and instead ask yourself why you have encountered certain situations. Identify the factual reasons and employ them to resolve issues. As a sage once taught, "A painting of a fish-less river is but a few ripples. Flower embroidery, though pretty, does not emit fragrance." If your practice is not correct in nature, you will see no improvement regardless of your effort to learn everything. Truthful practice brings truthful progress, which can be seen and felt.

The innate mind is neither clean nor polluted. However, Buddhism encourages the practitioner to see the mind from a pure perspective initially, so as to induce charitable thoughts. First, calm and balance your mind so as to keep the water from overflowing from the well. Observe your thoughts constantly, and peel away your ego layer by layer until you can locate the source of pureness.

The ones who constantly feel rejected are those who have endless worries; the ones who worry constantly tend to be those who repeatedly encounter problems and mistakes. Both fail to carry out self-reflection. Many who are confronted with adversities love to hold onto their own beliefs. Ironically, they are the least qualified to claim they are right. After all, what is the point of boasting that one is right despite being besieged by concerns and afflictions? If a person were truly walking on the right path, he would be happy in his life, with a pure mind free of worry.

Spiritual practitioners may not be the smartest people in the world, but they are courageous in facing their weaknesses and attempting a change in themselves. Many people who are otherwise logical and eloquent fail to understand themselves clearly. It can be said that the truth is right in front of our eyes. One's personality and habitual tendencies determine his being and his surroundings. Thus the ability to remain true to yourself will bring progress in your life, regardless of whether you practice any spiritual belief. However, the inability to face yourself or change yourself, even with constant spiritual practice, will take you nowhere. ✗

> Putuo Temple is situated on a beautiful island
> surrounded by the sea.
> The soaring guardian pine trees
> provide lofty canopies for the temple.
> A traveling monk always gets lost
> on his pilgrimage to the temple.
> He might as well meditate right where he is
> rather than searching for the temple.

# 9 CULTIVATE A BOUNDLESS MIND

The September golden chrysanthemums wave to the sun;
the cicadas by the river welcome the autumn coolness
 with a chirping song.
The withered grass in the moor seeks company
from the bright moon;
Hun Shang and Shih Te scratched each other's back.

## One Existence Cannot Create Another

A sentient being will not be able to transcend the constraints of time and space until he ceases his obsession with changing phenomena. The Chinese word for the physical world, *shijian,* is composed of two characters. The character *shi* means time, and *jian* means space. Indeed, attachments are the authors of time and space. These two concepts emerge the moment any attachment arises in the impermanent mortal. Instantly, the sentient being is held by the constraints of time and space.

The empty mind is the source of all phenomena, and it encompasses everything. All dharma is conceived from the emptiness of the Mind. This is a concept that is difficult for Western civilization to accept. Science is the material manifestation of the Western belief system. It is a pillar of science that only things of physical existence can construct, observe and sense other physical existences. Under this notion, the observation of all phenomena is made with the assumption that the observer remains the same at all times. In this dualistic system of logic, emptiness and existence are distinctions based on contrast. There is no reconciliation between the two.

Phenomena are interrelated. This relationship between one existence and another is only the correlation between one group of phenomena and other phenomena, in which both are parts of the Collective. This relationship between the parts of the Collective cannot be a causal one, however, because things that are created do not have the ability to create.

It is false to suppose that one existence can produce another existence. This idea is rooted in dualism but not in the non-dualistic nature of Mind and matter. Buddha said that the obsession with phenomena is an obstacle to the pursuit of enlightenment. When a person is fixated on phenomena, he or she falls into the mistaken belief that one existence can create another. This belief prevents a person from understanding the transcendental existence of emptiness. It obstructs his experience of the actualization of phenomena from the empty mind. For example, when you encounter a person who is doing something you dislike, you might question his or her intent. You might even feel compelled to lay blame, thinking that his or her action has caused your reaction. The truth is that the whole incident is a phenomenon manifested from your mind.

Many conditions are involved in the process of creating a phenomenon, so a single condition alone cannot foster the phenomenon's occurrence. It is comparable to how our physical bodies comprise billions of cells that are interrelated and mutually dependent. No single organ, such as a kidney or the heart, is responsible for affecting the rest of the body. Modern medicine may suggest that a patient's general health is at risk solely because of his heart condition, but this statement is incorrect.

Consider the heart as an example. When someone dies, the heart stops beating because the pulse has been created by functions from the innate mind. It is impossible for the heart, which is a created phenomenon, to initiate a pulse. In other words, a created phenomenon—in this case, the heart—does not have the ability to affect the kidney. The reason the heart and kidney are both unhealthy is that they are created with negative energy from the mind. Even though the heart and kidneys are correlated, one is not the creator of the other. The relationship between the two is mutually dependent, given their respective relationships with the mind. Therefore, it does not necessarily follow that certain negative factors in the heart will lead to an unhealthy kidney.

Physical existences are created. All existing energy, even the most subtle thought, is created. When the mind initiates a negative thought, it not only affects the mind but also causes the entire body to suffer from negative energy. An individual thought is only a tiny part of what is created by the mind. A person who does not understand this principle will claim that negative thoughts cause poor health. In fact, the relationship between one's thoughts and health is correlative but not causal.

A dualistic perspective leads to a life that is limited by superficial phenomena. By splitting into halves what the mind generates as a whole, one creates duality. A problem or a difficulty cannot be resolved by dealing with the correlations among existences, because it treats the symptoms instead of the root cause.

Adversities occur in accordance with the mind. The mind creates in a certain way, and then causality and phenomena manifest in a certain way. To change phenomena, we must alter the way the mind initiates effects. Given the emptiness of the mind, where would the starting point be for a person to change the way the mind creates phenomena? I have previously introduced, for the sake of explanation, the concept of changing the mind through changing thoughts. In fact, the change of a thought indicates that the effect of the mind has been transformed, just as the phenomenon it creates has been transformed.

Given the deep attachment to our physical bodies, we would naturally question the possibility of transforming phenomena through the mind. It is possible because, when the mind initiates different thoughts, it actually changes the way it functions and thus creates different phenomena. Therefore, physical existences and relationships within the whole will be altered accordingly. One should not simply isolate facts. The use of the body is merely an individual incident out of the wholeness of phenomena.

A person's intention to resolve issues is a creation of the mind, as are the movement of his or her body, the process of resolving issues and the result of such a process. As the mind induces various functions in a constant, consistent manner, it constitutes the continuous changes in thoughts, body, environment and relationships. When the result of the entire process is manifested by the mind, we call it the completion of the change process. The process of resolving a problem is, in fact, a manifestation of various functions of the mind.

This is a profound concept and a critical one to be grasped.

Humans are convinced that phenomena exist beyond their own existence and that one existence can create or affect another. However, this understanding is dualistic and impermanent. All phenomena follow the lead of the mind. To reach this level of spirituality, a person must be enlightened. The unenlightened know no better than to pursue, observe and understand one existence in the context of another. In other words, they create phenomena with a mind that is polluted by the ego.

Human beings constantly feel the changes in their bodies. At every stage in their lives, they impose onto themselves the concept of "I." By labeling themselves as handsome, beautiful, happy, sad, young, old, weak or healthy, they unconsciously create a self-identity that remains unchanged. This unchanging self-identity, however, is simply an illusion.

Ordinary people, being unaware of the true emptiness of the mind, attach their identity to phenomena created by the mind. They constantly identify themselves with the emotions they feel. According to Buddha, there is a being within a person that can only reveal itself when the person's mind is free of any thought, whether positive, negative or neutral. Once you find this being in yourself, you will find the true master of your life.

The relationship between the phenomenon that occurs this moment and the one that takes place in the next is not one of cause and effect. Instead, the relationship is determined by the direction in which the mind functions. A human being who is obsessed with phenomena will not be able to discover his or her identity once he or she is isolated from phenomena. Confusion will predominate. The patriarchs once said, "From where does birth come? To where does death lead?" Thoughts and energies in the body continually and simultaneously emerge and fade. So, what do the thoughts and the body have as their destination?

No one has an idea of what the Mind is unless he is awakened. He has no way to track the ultimate source of the changing phenomena. However, he can still assess his degree of delusion by observing the phenomena around him. He can also identify the direction in which he must strive forward. Everyone wants to encounter favorable situations and forego adversities. However, we must first understand that all environments, whether good or bad, are created by the Mind and manifested from the Mind. We must let go of the ideology that our fixation to phenomena will bring forth a positive change. The obsession with phenomena will only complicate the situation.

## "First, Loosen with Calmness, Then Extricate with Wisdom"

Buddhism focuses on the goal of transcending the Three Realms, thus signifying the end of birth and death. The physical world is a world of phenomena. The source of the world lies beyond the physical. The physical world is one of birth and death, thus representing the confines of all phenomena and activity. The phrase "birth and death" describes the nature of the change of phenomena. The empty Mind, free of ego, is the source of all phenomena. Only by rediscovering the Mind can anyone be liberated from the present phenomena.

Facts are the phenomena that take place in the present moment.

*-en: mind manifests into what become experiences*

Some people think that facts are predetermined by fate, but others think they are created by God. If it is true that predetermined fate is the sole cause of the events in life, we have no choice but to accept it. Because we do not know how to change it, we can only wait for good luck to come. If the adversities are sent from God, we can only pray that God will amend the situation. Zen, however, is based on a simple idea: The Mind is the creator. Our own experiences are exactly the results of our own doing. They are manifestations of the innate Mind. *If we can think from the pure mind, we escape adversity*

You should accept adversities as they come. Do not define them or isolate them in any way. Find out the root cause of why these facts exist so that the current problematic situation can be removed. If you are able to identify and solve a problem, it indicates that you have correct understanding. If you are unable to resolve the issue, however, you must amend your understanding. Any effort to deal with phenomena defined by your own understanding will be a waste of time unless you identify the source of phenomena. Consider it this way: When the mind deviates from the pureness, the phenomena induced will also indicate a distance from the optimal condition. How is it possible to eliminate the deviation in the phenomena with a mind that is biased?

Everything is created by our mind. The only way to change phenomena in a gradual but fundamental way is to guide the mind to produce different thoughts. By fixing your own internal issues, your relationships with family members and other people will change and your spirituality will be enhanced. For example, calm parents always have well-behaved children. This is because the two

*that we'd encounter the ability to change + transcend... isn't that what good wants*

*Fate brings events, and its then predetermined*

*But if God knows our thoughts he allows us to change where its needed*

*If*

parties share a similar energy. When it comes to parenting, "actions speak louder than words." Instead of giving your children speech after speech on the importance of obedience and hoping they will understand and accept it, you might as well devote your energy to improving yourself and enhancing your thoughts. That way, your family environment and family relationships will improve. Remember, when your children are not listening to you, it is because you lack the corresponding spiritual condition to bring forth the desired phenomena.

Some people complain with frustration that even as they improve spiritually their spouses remain the same. This is not correct. If they truly make progress within themselves, the environment around them will change accordingly. Therefore, the only way to change phenomena is to ensure a constant spiritual progression. You are the center of your world, so naturally the quality of your world will be enhanced as soon as you make progress in your life. A pure mind reflects pure phenomena, and a positive mind manifests a positive physical appearance.

Buddhism explores the topic of "taking up the Mind's essence and functions." In other words, the mind is one with what it reflects. The essence of the Mind manifests all phenomena as a non-dualistic collective. The mind can contain all dharma. It reflects on all dharma in a unitary way. To "take up the Mind's essence and function" is to promote the pure dharma of the mind through spiritual cultivation and attainment of the Way. In fact, at each moment every human being assumes the essence and function of the Mind, but the one who is burdened with attachments is ignorant of this. He is unable

Chapter 9

to step away from his own undesirable karma.

Most people are confused because they are not yet awakened. They lack the courage and ability to take up the responsibility for their lives, so instead they give excuses by saying, "It is none of my business," "The problem is not up to me," or "It is totally the fault of other people." People must completely submit to everything that comes into their lives. Whether a person is confused or awakened, ultimately the innate Mind's essence of function has equal capacity, even though it leads to different karma because the individual creates different realities. Your ignorance is responsible for the creation of your life, so you must take responsibility.

You must learn to abide with the mind in peace as you face the reality of each moment in life. You should distance yourself from grumbling and accept the facts as they occur from one moment to the next. Unless you do so, attachments will form, which will in turn create more afflictions. Moreover, the reasoning behind the acceptance of reality will affect the result of how you handle the issue. If your intention to submit to reality is not completely pure, the result will deviate from the truth.

Some Buddhist practitioners, after taking up spiritual practice, feel obliged to say that everything in their lives is due to the karma they deserve. Even though they seem to be confident in this regard, they still show dissatisfaction and unwillingness in life. They accept the reality because they are forced to do so, but their submission to reality is superficial. When a person such as this is faced with a predicament, he may comfort himself by saying that every experience is his mind's own doing. Unfortunately, such a statement does not necessarily represent his actual opinion, nor does it mean he has accepted the reality. The sincere acceptance of reality can be signified by a peaceful mind. The effects of a peaceful mind—such as calm, gentle speech and careful observation—will gradually eliminate attachments and bring forth a spiritual progression.

We must change our thoughts in order to amend the direction in which the mind functions. A factory can, at the most, maintain the same maximum production capacity when the facilities and equipment remain unchanged, but it cannot manufacture a new product. Life can only be transformed through the change of thought and the elimination of habitual thinking and attachments, which will in turn create favorable conditions.

The purification of the mind is the prerequisite for the practice of Buddhism. Regardless of whether the purpose of your practice is to improve your spirituality and achieve liberation from afflictions, or simply to gain success, wealth or fame, you must first purify the mind. Wisdom comes from a clear understanding of causality, without which any effort will only cause more frustration and future complications. A limited mind can only yield limited accomplishment. Closed-mindedness exists because the ideological structure of the mind has been so firmly established that it is difficult to open the mind. You must first loosen the ideological structure in your mind so that spiritual practice can be pursued.

An ancient saying goes like this: "First, loosen with calmness, then extricate with wisdom." People's attachments and troubles are so deeply rooted that they are like nails firmly hammered into the mind. We must first loosen the habitual tendency through meditative calm and then completely eliminate it through wisdom. For example, the absence of a response to mental chatter in meditation is a method of loosening the attachment in the mind, whereupon we realize the pure Mind itself and the attachment is ultimately eliminated through wisdom. To recognize the stars in the sky, we must first clear our eyes of any dust. Sakyamuni was enlightened as he gazed at the stars in the sky. That was the spontaneity of the moment of his enlightenment. At that moment of enlightenment, the dust of ignorance was removed from his mind. Therefore, it is said that one must remove the dust from his mind in order to realize the innate Mind.

The goal of Buddhist practice is to expand the mind to its full capacity. When we let go of our attachments, the mind expands. The more expansive the mind is, the more broadly and deeply we can understand the causality in everything. Thus there will be greater potential for success in life. The essence of existence is boundless. When the mind is as wide as emptiness, it can encompass all aspects of reality. Ego attachment limits the mind, so it cannot encompass the entirety of mind-made reality.

Once upon a time, a young man wrote a letter to his father who was an official for the imperial court. In the letter he told his father that their neighbor had built a wall that encroached upon their land. The father wrote in response, "A letter from you carrying no news but a note about a wall; what significance does a few lost inches have? You still see the Great Wall with all its magnificence; however, the almighty Qin Emperor is long gone."

It is indeed an invaluable thing that the official was so open-minded that he felt no desire to pursue the issue. Such open-mindedness, however, is something that many self-claimed practitioners cannot accomplish. The more open the mind is, the more merit it will receive. The mind, being innately empty, has infinite capacity. Unfortunately, people tend to narrow the mind with attachments and thus limit their perspective. A limited mind can only embody limited merits. Creations out of the habitual tendencies of the ego will be restricted by the limited capacity of such a mind.

## Unveiling Buddha's Understanding to Liberate All Sentient Beings

The goal of practice is to find our true home in life. Our well-being is assured when all the circumstances and experiences in life are settled in a true refuge. Well-being cannot be established merely by caring for the physical body through a healthy diet and adequate sleep. Well-being includes everything encompassed by the mind, which is beyond the ego's limited sense of existence in this earthly realm. This great well-being is that of the entire dharma realm, but it can only be established through our inner effort. To establish this great well-being, we must first identify the source of life.

Thoughts and physical bodies are only transitory aspects in the life of the sentient being. If the purpose of life is based on an impermanent thought or the physical body, in which a person chases after impermanent phenomena created by the mind, the foundation of his life will be unstable. The innate mind has limitless function, which in turn produces boundless life phenomena. If we become established upon the source of life, our lives will be infinite and eternal. Therefore, life should manifest from the Mind.

Stability, in this context, does not mean confinement. A stable mind is calm and pure. The nature and function of the innate mind are such that it is free of ego. Without ego, afflictions vanish. The mind is not mature and stable until a person reaches this state. The innate mind, free of ego, is peaceful and pure. As long as it is not disturbed, the innate mind will remain at peace. Once the innate mind is revealed, peace will dwell within, whether he is in action or at rest. Subsequently, a person in this state can enjoy a peaceful sense of well-being wherever he is, without having to rely on the tranquility of his surroundings.

Some experience pain and suffering in the mind even when they live a quiet, simple lives. This is because their unsettled minds are incapable of controlling their thoughts. When a person uses the formless mind—which is peace in itself—to pursue turbulent thoughts, environments and personal relationships, the mind becomes disturbed. It is unavoidably true that life is short and phenomena change constantly. However, we need not pursue them. Let them be, as they come and go. Enlightenment comes from the discovery of the ultimate source of life. Only after we find and master our own minds can we use it properly. Without such mastery, we are subject to an endless cycle of reincarnation.

The state of mind determines the environment that is manifested in life. Therefore, when the mind is imperfect the external environment is also imperfect. Considerable effort is needed in order for the practitioner to take responsibility for every phenomenon in his life, because he is the one who brings upon himself his appearance, his ill health and his relationships. The one who is wise can recognize, through the observation of objective facts, what must be amended. Such an individual does not view reality through the lens of his own attachment.

People often ask why bad things happen to good people. Everything comes to pass according to the eternal law of causality. If such people were truly perfect, they would not have met bad people or had bad experiences. The relationship between human beings and their experiences is like the relationship between two gears that mesh with one another. The two match precisely.

The one who has limited mind capacity is not up to Buddhist practice. Everything there is to see, hear and feel is born from the mind, and all that arises from causes and conditions has been created by the mind. Thus, everything is within our responsibility. In fact, there is no way other than to take the world upon yourself, because you are uniquely you; your reality is uniquely your creation. The minds of most people are so confined that they segregate the wholeness of phenomena into individual partitions. This is the way they twist the truth and avoid responsibility for their karma. They attribute their interpersonal relationships and everything in their lives to the external world, but there is really nothing external!

The innate mind is empty. When all of existence can be established within the mind of emptiness, there is true peace. In that state, peace will fill the mind regardless of the calamity that surrounds it. Even the occurrence of a landslide, earthquake or tsunami will not shake the mind, because these phenomena are recognized as merely reflections of the Mind. When every matter takes place as it happens and everything is settled as is, a person will find the true refuge upon which his life can be established because he has allowed all existence to return to where it belongs. Therefore, we should let phenomena belong to phenomena or, in others words, settle phenomena back into the formless mind. If one mistakes his or her insignificant body and thoughts as his or her true self and sees our environment as solely being that which is external, the mind will not be at peace because it cannot embrace all the phenomena it encounters.

According to the classic scriptures of Buddhism, "All Buddhas and saints appear upon the world for the sake of a great matter." So, what is this great matter? It is to unveil Buddha's understanding, demonstrate it, enlighten it and become one with it. What does it mean to unveil Buddha's understanding? Buddha is the Mind, and the dharma of the Mind is the understanding of Buddha. Therefore, to unveil Buddha's understanding is to reveal the understanding of the Mind and cultivate the realization that the pure, egoless mind is Buddha. Ordinary people hold a dualistic, paradoxical perspective that constantly fluctuates between the subjective and the objective. Given this perspective, what belongs to me is mine and what belongs to you is yours. Everything is exclusively defined and incompatible with any other thing.

Given the perspective of a Bodhisattva, one is sick when all sentient beings are not well because energies are interrelated and the causes and effects are inseparable. The Mind pervades the entirety of the great void, and its manifestation is one great whole, without the distinctions of east, west, north and south. Unfortunately, ordinary people distinguish themselves from others; they are indifferent to the suffering of others. This isolated view of reality is built upon ideas such as the self versus "other" and right versus wrong. Unable to eradicate the ego, people with this view fail to utilize the pure mind to embrace all emptiness. As a result, their minds are dissected into many pieces.

The only way to escape afflictions and worries and then become one with all sentient beings is to unveil Buddha's understanding. Your trouble is the trouble common to sentient beings. Your delusion is the delusion common to sentient beings. To become one with all sentient beings is to dissolve all dualistic concepts and paradoxes into the Mind. A sage said, "One is all; all is one." The Mind is one that encompasses everything. None can escape this "one." The person who is not awakened holds an ordinary understanding of duality. If you try to live in this boundless, ever-evolving universe with such a limited mind, you are bound to suffer many setbacks and afflictions.

An attachment is like a black hole, absorbing all of a person's energy and emotions. The more attachments he maintains, the more black holes there will be in his universe. When all energies are drained into the conflicts of the self and "other," and right and wrong, his life will be plagued with pain. The fewer black holes someone has, the more freedom he has. When thoughts arise from the innate mind, the thoughts will induce, from the mind, the corresponding energy that allows events to happen in certain ways. How can we prevent undesirable outcomes in life? The only way to do it is to cease the generation of negative thoughts.

The one whose mind is illuminated sees light; the one whose mind dwells in darkness sees darkness. The ancient literati were known for their sentimentalism. Their emotions fluctuated greatly, and their life journeys were dramatic. Thoughts tend to gather around attachments, which set the direction in which the mind tends to function. It is not easy for the mind to separate its functioning pattern from the attachment, which is why we compare attachments to black holes. When your energies are guided in the direction of attachments, your worries intensify. It is commonly said that a cat has nine lives. However, it has also been said that "worries can kill a cat." If you are obsessed with attachments and worries, there will be many obstacles.

It is useless to think about why certain events occur. The moment a person changes his mind, his so-called fate and world are altered. Change does not come from the external, but instead it must take place within. The wise one cultivates his mind, whereas the fool deals with his environment.

## The Emperor Who Governs with the Dao Enjoys Peaceful Borders

I often tell my students that altering their own thoughts and actions is the fundamental way to resolve concerns. Many students in turn tell me that the implementation of change within is more easily said than done. Life is not a multiple-choice question that allows you to choose what you want. You have no choice but to resume responsibility for your life. If you do not let go of burdens and worries, they will follow you. If you do not know how to change, you will always be stuck with the old self.

An open mind allows a person to establish his or her life. The mind of an enlightened person is as vast as the void. The unenlightened person, unable to locate the mind and forego attachments, is haunted by trouble wherever he goes. Even heaven cannot serve as a haven from troubles. Even if you should make it to heaven, you may not be able to stay there for long. Many people tell me that they cherish the clean, quiet environment of a monastery. However, if they were given the opportunity to live in the monastery they probably could not bear the lack of entertainment, the vegetarian diet, the solitude and the withdrawal from the liberty they enjoy back home. Many do not last longer than a few days.

Humans have human problems; no one is exempt. However, different people have different issues. Let us suppose that you are an accountant, and all you see every day are invoices, money and balance sheets. Naturally, all you think about are accounts receivable, accounts payable, account balancing and account reconciliation. Issues in life take forms depending on who you are, and the people around you are mirrors for reflection. Your association with a stubborn person indicates there is also stubbornness in you. Your relationship with a compassionate person reflects the seed of compassion in you. This is how karmic causality works.

If you are troubled by someone who is not applying himself to the practice, it indicates that you are not without indolence, even though you may seem diligent on the surface. Every person and situation around you is simply acting out the drama within your mind. Whatever is in you, it is acted out in your life. Energies interact. A Chinese idiom says, "Dragons are born of dragons, while phoenixes conceive phoenixes. The offspring of mice will always know how to dig holes." This demonstrates the interconnection of human relationships.

The proper handling of troubles in the mind ensures the resolution of life's issues. People and events are projections of our own minds. People serve as actors for one another's inner dramas—in other words, I become your project and you become mine—because of the so-called shared karma. Unless we identify the foundation of life, our spiritual practice will lack focus. The foundation of life is everything we possess at this moment, including our appearance, thoughts and personal relationships.

The Mind—being that of Buddha and Bodhisattva—is pure and wise. It is free of worry and pollution. So, naturally Buddha and Bodhisattva dwell in the same realm. Human appearances lack the dignity that is possessed by Buddha or Bodhisattva. Human minds are not as pure; they are tainted with many worries. Thus, they do not dwell in the same realm as Buddha and Bodhisattva. However, humans have not degraded to the level of ants, so human life is different from that of the insects.

Our surroundings are the backdrop for the stage of the mind. When there is abundant merit, the backdrop is beautiful. The landscape of the Pure Land is magnificent. However, the human world possesses many defects due to the limited capacity of the human mind. The plays of the human mind are often complex tragedies because of the complicated, turbulent nature of the mind.

It is easier to grow spiritually when we perceive the mission of our life journey as a process of mutual learning and support. One might say he would be carefree if he could be free of people in his life, such as his spouse or children. The truth is that a solitary life is not without worry, either. Ultimately, worries do not come from the external; instead, they are born from the mind. Problems occur when the mind is not pure and is therefore incapable of directing itself.

A sage used the following verse to illustrate the correct attitude in regard to the external environment: "Treat the conflict of right and wrong as if they are a passing breeze; Do not seek differences and similarities among dualities; In order to withstand the temptation of the eight worldly winds; Settle your mind like the true void." From a karmic point of view, no one in this world could take advantage of others or allow them to be taken advantage of. If someone does take or gain unfair advantage, it is due to the karma that has been accumulated in past lives. The causality of karma is so complex that even the most righteous judge will not be able to sort everything out, but it is absolutely just. Buddha does not judge. The Buddha never discusses right and wrong. Instead, the Buddha teaches that all dharma is rooted in the mind; that it is dependently arising through causes and conditions. Once we elevate ourselves through spiritual cultivation, worldly conflicts will naturally dissolve.

Causes and effects intertwine in various historical events that play out in endless dramas of revenge. It is more important that we understand how to solve human problems than that we try to pass judgments. Human perspectives on historical events change with time and circumstances, but the karmic law of causality remains the same. Therefore, human ethics should be based on the idea that each individual takes responsibility for his own creation. This is the highest standard of morality. If we impose our personal opinion on the law of causality, the conflict of right and wrong will arise.

It is said that "even the most unbiased judge cannot resolve domestic issues." However, the law of cause and effect will naturally ensure that each person takes up his or her share of the responsibility. When a person attains this perspective, he will have peace of mind. For instance, you would be better off working hard to earn money instead of losing sleep over the money you are owed by others. Ancient Zen masters always focused on doing the right thing in the moment, and they ignored everything else. This approach to solving problems goes directly to the fundamental principle that all dharma is born from the mind. A peaceful mind therefore ensures a peaceful world. A sage once said, "An emperor who governs with the Dao enjoys peaceful borders. There would be no need to have the thousands of miles of the Great Wall built."

Any discussion of causality spanning the past, present and future refers to the indivisible interpenetration of the infinite dimensions of space and time. Energy from every phenomenon, in every moment, infiltrates the immensity of time and space. Consequently, the true relationship of causality is extremely complex and far beyond our understanding. Buddhism introduced, for the sake of convenience, a linear concept of time—namely, the past, present and future—in order to explain the change in phenomena. Some might think they have done no wrong to others in their lives, but still their lives are full of adversity. They conclude that the world is unfair. It is really hard to say whether these people have indeed wronged no one, since they do not know how many others they have hurt or killed in their past lives. They must conduct self-reflection through pain, sickness, affliction, difficulties and trials in order to realize that it is their responsibility to face these hardships. After all, no one ever comes across what is not rightly his.

Excessive thinking will not help, but an unthinking person might as well be made of wood or rock. A human's ability to think can be a source of problems. When someone is told not to worry about things too much despite his suffering and pain, he tends to worry all the more despite being advised not to. If he really cannot stop thinking, he should at least think about or contemplate the truth of the Mind, because therein lies the opportunity to obtain freedom from suffering. To gain access to spiritual freedom, he should contemplate the dharma. If his mind is occupied with selfish concerns and pain, he might as well not think at all.

Buddha, when he attained the Way, gained wisdom, merit, perseverance, charity and supernatural powers. These were the accomplishments achieved through spiritual practice, which he demonstrated to mundane beings. Buddha taught us that we must master our own minds, and this is the perspective every sentient being must attain. Unless someone first realizes his or her innate nature, any spiritual practice will be in vain even if that person gains supernatural powers or longevity. Every accomplishment will vanish, eventually. Only true emptiness is eternal.

The mind should remain empty and return everything to the Mind, in order to let go of attachments. Once the Mind is realized, a person is able to abide in a state free of ego. To function with a mind free of ego is to unveil the Buddha's understanding. Because the innate mind is empty, its function and manifestations are inseparable from its innate purity, whereby all is embraced in totality without the distinction of inner, outer, subject, object, self, other, and right versus wrong. To have the ability to master this way of functioning with the Mind is to demonstrate the Buddha's understanding. To realize Buddha's understanding is to realize that the mind's functions are inseparable from the nature of emptiness of the Mind. Lastly, to actualize the Buddha's understanding means that, as the pure mind functions, these functions return to the mind. In other words, every thought is born from the mind, inseparable from the source, and returns to its innate essence.

Dharma is born from the mind and eventually returns to the mind. In other words, it is unveiled from the mind and is ultimately returned to the mind. Interestingly, the unveiling and return of the dharma occur simultaneously. In other words, the moment the mind creates functions, those functions vanish amid the pure nature of the mind. Thus, the unveiling and the actualization of Buddha's understanding complete a concurrent process. When the mind is creating phenomena, awareness is present. If the internal awareness is free of ego, the external awareness can embrace all dharma. Then, these types of awareness are as one. In this state of mind, we will realize the Buddha's understanding. When the pure mind is functioning, every phenomenon induced will harmonize with the totality of the mind's creation, being inseparable from the source. This is the state in which we demonstrate Buddha's understanding.

A sage said, "Without a mind that is as capacious as the universe, how can one aspire to be a saint?" The awakening is the foundation of spiritual practice, and practice is the foundation of spiritual accomplishment. A person's potential to gain sainthood lies in the mind. The moment he recovers his primordial mind, his ego will be eradicated. This egoless mind is where the seed of sainthood is planted. The ancient phrase of "nurturing the sacred seed" refers to the cultivation of a newly awakened mind.

One cannot establish his life without an awareness of the innate mind. If your mind is not as open and vast as the void, you will perceive that creations on earth exist separately from your own existence. Consequently, the mind will not be able to encompass them. With this major fault in the mind, you will not be able to end samsara. Only a fully recovered primordial mind can encompass everything and acknowledge that everything manifested in that person's life—all thoughts, the body and environment, whether desirable or not—is part of his true self. Through this perspective, the mind will gain peace.

All enlightened Zen masters teach the same principles. Buddha descended into the mundane world to teach mankind to realize his innate mind. To fulfill the pure functionality of the mind, we must not be obsessed with the phenomena generated by the mind. Phenomena are impermanent. They emerge from the mind and instantly vanish into the mind. This is the essential teaching of the Buddha. All Buddhist teachings have originated from this principle for the purpose of guiding mankind toward enlightenment.

We must understand, whether we are enlightened or not,

that every experience in every moment is karma reflected from the mind. Our karma is brought forth by our mental structure, attachments and habitual tendencies in the mind. Because we are responsible for casting every character in the play of our mind, we must accept them calmly. It is the most fundamental law, and the highest moral standard of life, that we must own up to every karmic consequence of our own doing.

One must actively cultivate his mind through the gradual elimination of worries, attachments and habitual tendencies in order to create a new outlook on life. This is not only the ruling principle for spiritual practice but is also an overall guideline for life. Transcendence from the mundane world lies in the ultimate freedom of the mind. Do all that is charitable, but do not be obsessed with charity. To liberate the mind, you must first contemplate the cause and source of phenomena. Trace phenomena back to their source. Do not use one phenomenon to solve another because, based on the law of causality, what is created cannot create. Any behavior against the law of causality is counterproductive.

Very few worship at the old temple,

whereas the grand temple is filled with

the fragrance of incense.

 As no one recognizes the significance of

the pure functions of the mind,

the head monk is obliged to preach about

the east and the west.

# 10 A MIGHTY SKYSCRAPER RISES FROM THE GROUND

The purity of the white lotus in the east

cannot be concealed by the water.

The glory of the red lotus in the west

reveals from its half-open blossom.

The same can be said of the yellow lotus and the green lotus

in the south and the north.

Yet, where is the mind that appreciates the lotus' beauty?

## The Transformation of Negative Thoughts
## Can Save All Sentient Beings

Mastery of the mind is the main goal of Buddhist practice. To achieve this goal, the mind must be pure and free from attachments. Delusions, worries and attachments obscure the mind's potential by polluting its tranquility. Therefore, you should not practice Buddhism in the hope of gaining some supernatural power. Practitioners may have supernatural experiences in the process of meditation, such as seeing certain phenomena, hearing certain sounds, experiencing various physical changes, and witnessing light and energy, but these experiences should not be the goals of spiritual practice.

It is true that some people who have supernatural powers are still, to their great frustration, unable to handle their own suffering and vexations. Their minds are too easily swayed by worries, attachments and delusions. It is in such a state that a defiled mind—a mind that has not been awakened—becomes trapped.

The mind is the element that determines whether someone would be born into the Realm of Buddha, the Realm of Devils, the Realm of Asura or anything in between. When the mind continuously produces compassionate thoughts, it will naturally resonate with the realm of the compassionate. However, if the mind continues to generate negative thoughts, worries, jealousy, malicious thoughts and discriminative thoughts, it will gradually descend into the Realm of Devils. When the mind contemplates its emptiness and the intrinsic awakened nature, that person will gradually resonate with the way of the saints.

Ordinary people have many delusions and attachments that conceal light, pureness and wisdom of the mind. The goal of Buddhist practice is to eliminate the delusions and attachments, because they are obstacles to a free mind. Every thought is a realm. Sentient beings are epitomized in a single thought; accordingly, introspection and the gradual transformation of negative thoughts are the means to awaken all sentient beings. You must take responsibility over your realm. You must discern, tame and transform your thoughts. This, in Buddhist terms, is the liberation of self-nature. A mind that is not able to convert thoughts is a mind of ignorance, attachment and delusion. If your mind is not disciplined, you will not be able to enjoy free will and action.

The effect of spiritual practice does not depend upon how long you can maintain a meditative posture or how many volumes of scriptures you can study. These are simply methodologies for practice. Neither is spiritual practice aimed at sighting the light, spirits or Buddha. The foothold of a Buddhist practice should be the resolution to reveal the purity and wisdom of the mind and thereby restore its liberty.

Because we are fully aware of the negative effect that worry has, we must learn to shatter any worry as soon as the mind generates it. Restore your mind to its innate peaceful tranquility by disengaging any troubling thought. Thoughts are the food of character, and therefore an undetected thought of worry, attachment or anger will lead to a chain of undesirable thoughts that eventually develop into a negative personality.

The innate mind encompasses the true void and all realms: the Realm of Devas (Gods) and Heavenly Beings, the Realm of Asura, the Realm of Hungry Ghosts, the Hell Realm, the Animal Realm and the Human Realm. The mind is capable of all creations, so it is essential that we aspire to the right kind of creation. When the mind initiates a negative thought, it will feed energy into the Realm of Asura. An obsessive thought provides food for the realm corresponding to that attachment. A malicious thought gives livelihood to the Realm of Devils. A thought on the nature of true emptiness provides the abiding of arahats.

A practice must be built upon a solid foundation that begins with the practice of discerning, transforming, taming and purifying your thoughts. Although the future seems distant, every thought generated today serves as the source of nourishment for your eventual transformation. These thoughts will form the facts of the future. The more negative the thoughts the mind produces today, the more dominant the forces of negative existence will be in the future.

# mind must be its own master

The more compassionate the thoughts the mind generates now, the more likely you are to be elevated to a state of wholesomeness in the future. Ultimately, you are the creator of your world, so take charge and do what is right for your life. In the long journey ahead, you must learn to hold the mind accountable for its creation. A mind that is not its own master will guarantee the present suffering and even more adverse consequences in the future.

## Buddhist Practice Emphasizes One's Intentions

A practice begins with intention, which is of primary importance. First, you must identify the purpose of practice. Ask yourself: Why am I seated in the meditation hall? Why am I reading the scriptures? Why am I studying in the lecture hall? What is the purpose of all these actions? Is it because I want to improve myself? Do I want to learn because I want to overcome worries so that my mind can be its own master? Be sure to identify the purpose of your spiritual practice, and then adopt a method to observe, transform and elevate your thoughts. Lastly, eradicate your attachments and restore the mind to its pure, egoless state.

One's practice will lack a proper causal foundation unless there is a clearly defined goal. Your initial thought regarding spiritual practice serves as the seed for your spiritual growth. Therefore, a bad seed will yield an undesirable crop. Some come to the meditation hall intending to expand their social circles while learning some meditation on the side. This is an ill-intended practice, because it is not rooted in the transformation of vexations and thoughts.

A lay practitioner once visited our meditation hall. When asked who had referred her, she said that she had read about the meditation hall in a newspaper. When asked about her goal, she said she hoped to find a husband for herself by mingling with the many attendees here. Indeed, she put this thought into practice. Some business people also come to the meditation hall to look for potential clients. Others come with the intention of attaining supernatural powers and a sixth sense, with which they might see the past and the future. It will be difficult for them to make any improvement in their study, because their intentions are wrong.

We should practice Buddhism with the desire to build a positive karma, achieve liberation from afflictions, attain wisdom and pureness, and help ourselves as well as others. The proper intentions should be based upon the desire to overcome worries, free the mind, achieve enlightenment, reveal the innate nature of the mind, and develop compassion and wisdom.

Everyone arrives at the meditation hall through different connections, which evolve constantly. Some people may have started out because they wanted to transcend the cycle of life and death. However, due to the inability to transform habitual tendencies, attachments and worries in the mind, they lose sight of their original intention, start to regress and ultimately give up their practice. There are also those who do not come with a commitment to cultivation but come based on their admiration for the master's books. Perhaps they are drawn to the tranquil environment of the temple as a retreat. Nonetheless, they gradually start to be in tune with the dharma, whereupon they realize that cultivation expresses life as it should be. Then, they endeavor to advance themselves and transform their worries. These examples demonstrate that intentions can change.

An ill intention is like a false seed or the seed of a poisonous fruit tree. As the practitioner continues to meditate, contemplate doctrines and study the scriptures, he actually nurtures the false seed. He cannot let go of his obsession with fame, wealth and passion, and consequently he suffers from jealousy and confrontational relationships. Eventually, he will give in to temptations and craving. It is imperative for a practitioner to set a clear goal for meditation and chanting. Otherwise, he will not realize what seed he has nurtured and which spiritual path he has traveled.

The innate mind is plain and free of ego, but it can create all functions and generate various thoughts. Spiritual practice seeks to enlighten the mind through the elimination of attachment. If the light, wisdom and awareness of the mind is the sun, habitual tendencies are like the layers of dark clouds that conceal the sun. If the sunlight cannot penetrate the clouds, it will not be able to illuminate the world. The purpose of Buddhist practice is to dispel the clouds of habitual tendencies, layer by layer, and thereby reveal the pureness, light, awareness and wisdom of the mind.

The Sixth Patriarch Huineng instructed Zen Master Huiming that one must forego all thoughts and cease grasping phenomena in order to achieve enlightenment. To forego phenomena means we cease the pursuit of phenomena and appearances. We must clear the mind of all thoughts, whether good or evil; we must contemplate the identity of the one who is free of thought and then eradicate all attachments.

*meditation hall rules*

Let us consider our presence in the meditation hall. You should concentrate on calming and clarifying your thoughts, purifying the mind through inner illumination. Do not carry a rosary or scriptures. Do not chant. If there is a dharma talk, listen attentively and avoid counting rosary beads. Do not look around. If you become drowsy, try to stay awake. If random thoughts arise, try observing your thoughts closely. The mind is the source of all good and evil, and therefore you must tend the mind and master it in order to master your thoughts and life. The way to tend and manage the mind is to tend and manage your thoughts.

## Liberation Comes from the Mastery of the Mind

Zen Master Baizhang once said that the essence of Mahayana's dharma on instant enlightenment referred to the awakening of the innate mind. As we eliminate ignorance, attachments and other obstacles in the mind, we experience the innate mind, which transcends good versus evil, right versus wrong and "ego versus others." Master Baizhang taught his followers to "subdue all desires and settle all matters."

A sage taught, "As long as your mind is not attached to any phenomenon, there is no need to be bothered by being surrounded with them." Therefore, let go of your attachments and let what you see and hear be as they are. Do not pursue them with other positive or negative thoughts. To feel positive or negative means you are letting the mind function in a certain way that produces the feeling.

The goal of spiritual cultivation is to return to the innate nature of the mind. The goal is not to train the mind to generate thoughts, regardless of whether they are good or bad. Do not judge people or define things in life. If your mind generates thoughts based on the phenomena you encounter, it means there is an attachment to appearances. This tendency to attach forces the mind to generate thoughts constantly, leaving little time to search for its innate state of being.

Zen Master Baizhang taught that everyone must let go of what they see and what they hear. We must not pursue or become attached to any thought or phenomenon, "whether it is good or bad, of the world or beyond." In regard to all ideas and phenomena, we should not try to recall them or ponder them. Instead, we should inquire into our minds without grasping the world so that we can "relinquish the body and mind, and rest at ease." Once we let go of our mental tendencies and obsessions with regard to the physical body, we will experience in our body and mind a strong sense of freedom and comfort. When we reach this state, our "mind will be as still as a rock or a piece of wood, no longer trying to judge anything that happened with a follow-up thought." The mind will not react with an additional thought when it hears a sound or sees an event. This secondary reaction comes from the mind's habitual tendency. Why do we want to model the mind after rock and wood? It is because we want to counteract the strong tendency to react to people and situations. Feelings are relative and personal. Everyone has his or her own, unique feelings. Although never absolutely right, feelings are an inevitable part of life.

As human beings guide their minds to think in certain ways, they impose on themselves feelings in the same direction. Positive emotions originate from a thought that projects good feelings, whereas negative feelings come from a thought that induces negative feelings. These thoughts, which induce feelings, are deeply rooted in habitual tendencies. Feelings are personal, not universal. However, the mind's ability to create unique feelings is universal.

A mind that is "as undiscriminating as a rock or a piece of wood" is not a dumb mind but is one that turns toward its innate nature by withdrawing its habitual tendency to form attachments. "The mind that is free of action" is thoughtless and illuminating inwardly upon the source of thought. "When the ground of the mind is like the void, wisdom will naturally emerge." The scriptures describe the beautiful scene when wisdom emerges: "It is as if clouds clear up and reveal the sun."

"The mind that is free of action" means the mind is so peaceful and pure that it does not react to the environment, superficiality or vexation. When someone practices Zen by engaging hua-tou, he tends to the thoughtlessness that is the source of thought and even life itself. The moment a thought arises, it is not the source but the product. In other words, thoughts are the "actions" of the mind. The mind is formless, so its actions are thoughts and feelings. Therefore, the practice of tending to hua-tou means tending to the point where thoughts arise without being led astray by feelings or other thoughts. This is the meaning of a mind that is free of action.

The scripture states, "Withdraw from all pursuits of superficiality, greed, enmity, preference and demand. Then, filth will be cleansed. Emotions will end." Indeed, we must forego all superficial pursuits and raise no thought of cupidity, anger, propensity or imposition:

"Resist the strong temptation of desires. Avoid being shackled by senses and feelings. Stay clear of the confusion from varying environments." We are truly enlightened when we can let go of impure ideas, superficial pursuits, delusions and attachments, as well as flattering or slandering words from others, but also remain clear with respect to our thoughts.

We are liberated from the enchantment of a worrisome thought if and when we recognize the thought and choose to withdraw from it. Therefore, liberation comes when the mind is free to abandon its attachments and generate or not generate a certain thought at any moment.

The Fourth Patriarch Daoxin once asked his master, the Third Patriarch Sengcan, the way toward liberation. The Third Patriarch asked, "Who binds you?" The student Daoxin responded, "No one." The teacher continued, "If no one binds you, why are you asking for liberation?"

The mind is the source of all thoughts, but the mind is not free if it cannot control its thoughts. Anger, vexation, obsession and thoughts over existence, whether past or future, are creations of a limited mind. The origin of life is the true place where we can establish our lives. The source of life is the pure mind; it is the unattached mind, the mind free of worry and the mind free of conflict and dispute. We are liberated when we can return to the pure mind and abide there with ease.

A liberated mind can still function, but it is no longer manipulated and oppressed by its thoughts. Being upset or frustrated despite a deliberate effort not to be upset or frustrated shows that you are victimized by your thoughts. The same is true with anger, distress and obsession. When the mind is not free, you cannot be the master of your own life.

## There Is No Holy Way Other Than Letting Go of the Mundane

We must start with our thoughts in order to eliminate worries and transform feelings. In spiritual practice, we can certainly read a lot of literature and study many different methodologies, but the most essential element is to cultivate the mind by ensuring that every thought is compassionate, kind and, eventually, pure and awake. If your current thoughts are not yet up to these standards, all you need to do is transform them. This is the true practice. Certainly, a person who imagines there is some mystical shortcut is misguided. Under such a misguided assumption, he will not achieve anything regardless of how much literature he studies or how many pilgrimages he makes. These efforts would be like shooting arrows in different directions without ever hitting the target.

A person can talk the talk as much as he wants, but he must still walk the walk in very practical terms by starting from where thoughts arise in his own mind. Mind your thoughts in daily life, or all your efforts and study will amount to nothing. The more compassionate your thoughts are, the more accomplished your spiritual practice will be. The more negative your thoughts are, the closer you will be to the three realms of evil. If you attempt to calm the mind through discussion of the void, the totality of reality and enlightenment would be like trying to quell hunger by talking about food. Superfluous practice has no real meaning.

Zen Master Daowu, of the Tang Dynasty, once resided at Tianhuang Temple. A young man next door was a pastry seller who gave the Master ten pastries each day as a tribute. However, Master Daowu always took nine and returned the remaining one to the young man. He said, "I return this pastry to you as a blessing to your offspring." He thought to himself, "Every time I give my master ten pastries, he returns one to me with the same saying. There must be a reason he says that."

One day, he asked the master, "Teacher, the pastries are for you, so why do you return one to me?" The master responded by saying, "Those are your pastries. So, what is wrong with taking back one of them?" The pastries of which Master Daowu spoke represented what is in the mind, not the pastries in the literal and external sense. No matter where one is, the mind comes thus and goes thus. Coming and going are collectively the action of the mind. After the young man heard the answer, he decided to become a monk, following Master Daowu. The master said, "Because you value practice for merit and have firm faith in Buddhist dharma, I will ordain you as Chongxin, meaning 'faith.'"

A few years had passed since Chongxin became Master Wudao's disciple, but he felt that he had learned nothing. One day, he mustered his courage and asked his teacher, "Why is it that you have never given me any instructions on the mind dharma, even though I have been here so long?" Master Daowu answered, "I have thought you the dharma of the mind every day, haven't I?" Bewildered by the teacher's answer, Chongxin asked, "What was your teaching?"

Master Daowu replied, "I eat when you hand me food. I drink when you hand me tea. I nod when you greet me. When have I not taught you?"

Nodding, walking and drinking tea are all functions from the mind. Without the mind, how can these functions exist? From these functions we can learn of the mind. The action of serving the tea and the action of accepting the tea are both functions from the mind, as are greeting and nodding in response. When Chongxin heard the answer, he lowered his head and pondered it. Master Daowu then told him: "If you know, you know. If you continue to think, then you are going in the wrong direction." Once a person starts thinking, his mind will be influenced by the effect of thinking and lose track of the truth.

Chongxin was enlightened when Master Daowu told him, "If you see, it is right there; to contemplate already misses it." Realization is immediate. The mind is formless. To see it, we must seek out the point where thoughts arise as if trying to penetrate layers of clouds in order to see the sun. When we start to think, however, we fall into the trap of dualism. No matter the layer of cloud in which we dwell, the sun will remain obscured.

Chongxin, having been enlightened, asked his teacher how he should continue to learn the dharma. The teacher answered, "Let your innate nature be itself. Unfold freely with your karma. There is no holy way other than to let go of the mundane." Let your innate nature be itself and dwell within the pure mind, where thoughts are clear and in control. To unfold freely with your karma means that, under all circumstances, you will abide in the essence without disturbance, allowing the external conditions to unfold as they are.

People are often infuriated by political developments in the news. Under the influence of the news, their reckless minds prompt them to vent their angry criticism. A mind that is manipulated by phenomena and environment is not free but is instead rigid and prone to attachment. As long as negative emotions exist in the mind, a person is not free from the pursuit of external phenomena.

A mind that dwells in pureness is free and unrestricted. This does not mean the mind is not functioning; instead, it is functioning without the trappings of form. A sight no longer induces thought in the mind, and accordingly the mind is as clear as a mirror, reflecting all appearances. In abiding this way, a person can dissolve the negative karma of his past. If people, things and experiences can induce frustration and anger in a person's mind, he is no longer free as karma unfolds. Instead, he generates more thoughts and creates more karma.

It is acceptable to have happy feelings or worrisome feelings as long as we can refrain from indulging them. If someone is unable to withdraw emotions, it indicates that he is still habitually grasping appearances and samsara. "There is no holy way other than to let go of the mundane." Forego all delusions and you will attain sainthood. The mind will be pure when it abandons worry, attachment and binary opposition. If you try to attain purity of mind without letting go of these thoughts, the goal will not be achieved.

"Let your innate nature be itself. Unfold freely with your karma. There is no holy way other than to let go of the mundane." This Zen teaching points out the direction in which a practitioner should strive forward. A person can talk all the talk he wants, but unless he practices the basics his efforts will not amount to anything. Consider the phrase, "a skyscraper rises from the level ground." How can you elevate yourself to those lofty states of enlightenment as described in the scriptures and finally escape samsara? The answer is to mind your thoughts, transform them and elevate them.

Thoughts are the true manifestations of life. They are the foundation of phenomena and realms, as well as the basic building blocks of the mind's creation. They indicate the direction through which the mind functions. Therefore, you must base your practice on training your thoughts. This process includes the transformation of negative thoughts, worries and attachments. When this is accomplished, you will have a firm foundation for spiritually rewarding practice. Negative thoughts bring forth afflictions. It is a disservice to your practice to allow attachments in the mind to behave as they please.

Practice requires a correct intention, first and foremost. This intention comes from an understanding of your mind as well as its innately pure nature and liberty. You must not practice spirituality for the sake of wealth, fame, personal gain, marriage prospects or supernatural powers. Secondly, a firm foundation is essential to practice. Watch over every thought. Transform your thoughts and improve them. Daily practice is not a slogan. Instead, it requires the concerted effort to mind and transform your thoughts.

It is for one's best to own up to one's accountability,

lest one is forced to deal with it under the bat.

Linji and Deshan are the ministers of the family,

the ancient Buddha of Caoxi is the master.

# 11 PLAY THE PROTAGONIST IN THE STORY OF ENLIGHTENMENT

Zen contemplation is like rafting.

Rough whitewater diverts the route on the way.

 With rocks up front and waterfall at the back,

whosoever can go against the strong wave and strive to the end will be the champion.

## "All Beings Possess the Nature of Buddha and Nirvana": This Is Nothing to Gloat About

Buddhist scripture states, "All sentient beings possess Buddha nature." The phrase "all sentient beings" refers to phenomena and effects, which can be traced back to their origin. It is expressed as "all sentient beings possess Buddha nature" because no phenomenon can exist apart from its origin. Each minute and every second, our minds create and demonstrate various phenomena. We must bring along our karma on our life journey.

The principle that "all sentient beings possess Buddha nature" is significant, but at the same time it is insignificant. Why do I say this? It is because Buddha nature is our innate nature, whether we are aware of it or not. It is simply how life works. The reality that all beings possess an innate mind and the nature of Buddha sounds fantastic, but it actually is nothing worth gloating about. The good and the evil both possess this Buddha nature. All those who ascend to heaven and those who are doomed to hell have Buddha nature. Therefore, the impact this principle has on our life depends on how we make use of it.

Ordinary Buddhist practitioners suggest that Buddhism is different from or more sophisticated than other religions because of its doctrine that "all sentient beings possess Buddha nature." Whether it is different or the same, it depends on the perspective from which we consider the issue. Buddha nature, or the Zen term "innate mind," is something each and every human being has. It is possible for anyone to return to or attain the innate mind. Unfortunately, most people must first face the cold reality of karma.

Subtle thoughts manifest with subtle forms, and they are detectable only by the Buddha and Bodhisattva, whereas ghosts and devils are able to distinguish relatively gross, obvious thoughts. Imagine that the mind produces the thought to smile: This thought is subtler in comparison to the smile that appears on the face. The thought to smile is the subtle face of the mind, while the facial display of a smile is the grosser expression of the mind. Greater still are the relationships and environment around us.

The mind can function every moment and produce phenomena as self-expression. In fact, your thoughts, emotions, facial expressions, physical body and interpersonal relationships—as well as the entire universe—are egocentric illustrations. They are all expressions of your mind, and you live among these illustrations every day. Even if you do not think about the mind or the Buddha nature, and whether you are aware of the concept of the innate mind or not, you still use it at all times. Problems, suffering, enlightenment and spiritual attainment all come from the mind. Thus, the fact that "all beings possess the Buddha nature" is neither good nor bad. It is nothing to gloat about.

The fortunate aspect is that every sentient being has the ability to transform the current karma, given the choice to function better with the mind and manifest a better expression. Do not believe that the doctrine "all beings possess the Buddha nature" is superior to the doctrines of Western religions. Western religions suggest that the purpose of life on earth is to glorify God and that human beings are God's expressions. This philosophy parallels the Buddhist precept that all phenomena are illustrations of the Mind. When one makes spiritual progress, the Mind naturally manifests purity and light, which can be considered a form of glorification.

The mind possesses the functionality to form appearances. The effects created from this function cannot diverge from the actual function, because all dharma are inseparable from the Mind. In theory, no one can isolate himself from the origin of life, whether this origin of life is called God, the Mind or the Buddha nature. Each person's life is lived through this ability. His or her current situation, whether good or bad, is the manifestation of the mind. Spiritual cultivation is for the purpose of realizing the shortcomings of the way someone functions with the mind through phenomena.

People in the past spent relatively long periods of time on their spiritual practices. Whether a person practiced at home or in the temple, he or she would give the practice sincerity and solid effort, such as with routine meditation in the mornings and evenings. Their ideas and interpersonal relationships were purer, less complicated and more rooted in wholesomeness. Therefore, it was possible for them to attain spiritual enlightenment using a single method of practice. Modern practitioners do not put routine efforts into their practice. Instead, they may listen to one lecture a week and occasionally perform meditation, scripture study and chanting. The negative effects that build up in the course of daily life completely outweigh the efforts they put into their practices.

A person's effort in spiritual practice can be compared to his earnings, and negative karma is like his debt: Most people today earn very little money but accumulate a great deal of debt. As someone constantly generates negative functions from the mind, he takes out loans, which will have to be repaid in the future. When his income is less than his expenditures, his merits will gradually decrease. This may manifest in the form of poor health, dissatisfied relationships and financial difficulties. Moreover, wisdom will be dimmed and perceptions blurred. His ability to handle problems and make life decisions will be compromised. These examples are just some of the consequences of insufficient merit and wisdom.

Practice requires the establishment of a routine. Given the lack of the basic practices, a person's understanding of the mind will be limited as well. For the time being, we will set aside the question of whether "all beings possess the Buddha nature" is different from the concept of God in other religions. Instead, ask yourself whether you live a good life. What we need in life is not doctrine but practical application. The practitioners of the past were able to attain the Way within a lifetime because they diligently applied the teaching.

We must clearly identify our issues in reality. Isn't it foolish for someone to carry out spiritual practice while turning a blind eye to his problems in life? Ask yourself whether you are a person with compassion and integrity. Many people take pride in themselves, thinking they are doing just fine. However, when they consider things more deeply they realize that they would not have so much trouble if they were as good as they believed themselves to be. Most people's issues are similar in nature. A great deal of complacency about people's flaws is due to ignorance regarding their issues. Positive self-perception is often an illusion. Human karma and thoughts are combinations of positive and negative polarities. Therefore, it is imperative to closely examine a positive self-perception.

People often ask me, "Teacher, what are the problems with my practice? Why are people oblivious to their problems, afflictions, greed, anger and ignorance?" I reply that this question is already answered by the phenomena around them: Your reality already shows what your effort can produce. If the work you put into your spiritual practice is limited, how can you possibly say that you are unaware of any shortcomings in your spirituality? When faced with a difficulty, you must always remember that the trial is related to the thoughts and habitual tendencies in the mind. If someone does not even recognize the correlation between the two as well as the source of his problems, he is merely a muddle-headed simpleton to whom enlightenment is simply out of the question.

The one who does not know how he has reached his current circumstances is like a sleepwalker who has no idea how he ends up where he is. If a person does not know why he encounters difficulties, he might as well be a walking corpse. Such irresponsibility is not in harmony with the wisdom of Buddhist dharma. Your body cannot move by itself, nor can your karma be created by itself. Therefore, you must honestly admit that you are the one who has created your karma. Most people are unwilling to confront and accept their problems. The refusal to acknowledge problems is the biggest problem anyone has.

## Taking a Koan as Just Another Story Will Have No Impact on Your Spiritual Growth

Spiritual cultivation does not rely solely on your physical and visible work. More importantly, you must identify your inner faults by examining the phenomena in your reality. Practitioners who openly and verbally admit their wrongdoings and afflictions but do not sincerely dig to the roots of their problems cannot help themselves, because their actions are superficial. It is useless to admit your problems unless you proceed to correct them. When your thoughts and behavior are not mutually consistent, the deception to yourself and others will fail to bring forth real change.

People may assert that they are good and that they are unaware of any personal flaws. However, if they truly have so many compassionate thoughts, they would not be dwelling in the Realm of Human Beings. The mundane world is a school in which all the students are required to do pretty much the same assignments due to their greed, anger, delusion, arrogance and doubt. Someone can certainly have confidence in his integrity, confirmed by others' affirmations, but no one else's approval will help transform his karma, sickness and suffering.

The one who is enlightened has a solid foundation for calming the mind; for eliminating its afflictions and attachments. A mind that is haunted by vexation will find it difficult to use the dharma. In this case, any teaching that person follows or any method he uses would only be a culprit in the outward pursuit of dharma. No progress will be achieved until he has the proper emphasis in his effort. Therefore, observe your thoughts with a calm mind. Do not take it for granted that you are a decent person, that you work hard and that you have a good reputation. These compliments are games that belong to the mundane.

Meditation, chanting and scriptural study are certainly helpful. However, your practice should always focus on the transformation of perspective and personality, the purification of the mind, the reduction of personal disputes, honest self-assessment and a sincere effort to change.

The Zen koan and verses are beautiful and rhythmic. They are stories about enlightenment and the end of samsara. As inspiring as the koan and verses are, spiritual transformation depends on the fundamental effort to change the personality and break away from concerns and obsessions. If there is no change in either respect, these stories will only burden you. A koan can be beneficial to those who are strong enough to be accountable for their karma. For others, however, they are useless. The ancient wisdom states: "Buddhist practice requires one's strength and perseverance, with which one can act decisively in changing the mind. One heads straight toward the unsurpassed awakening and ignores all worldly controversies." Only with the above conviction, accountability, courage and spirituality can anyone benefit from scriptural teachings. Otherwise, the teachings will poison the spirit.

How can a person's spirit be poisoned when he listens to the teachings? It does appear very desirable to aspire toward enlightenment and the Way, as described in Zen scriptures. However, an obsession with the pursuit of enlightenment without the clear identification of personal issues is comparable to a bankrupt person who fantasizes about becoming a billionaire. The desire to pursue spiritual awakening is commendable, but truth will always be there. The failure to find the truth is a personal failing.

How can you benefit from lectures? First, you must start with the basic effort in practice. In other words, be patient, compassionate, kind and responsible to a certain degree. Without these basic characteristics, the fruit of enlightenment will remain too distant to attain. The Buddhist lectures will, in that case, be like watching the astronaut Neil Armstrong walk on the moon: Certainly it looks impressive, but one cannot relate it to everyday life.

A great example of a koan would be the one about Zen Master Shanzhao's nirvana. Lord Lihou, of Longfu, asked Master Shanzhao to become the abbot of Chengtian Temple. At the time, abbots were appointed by the government. When Lord Lihou sent an envoy to Fenyang to invite Master Shanzhao to the temple, the master responded by saying, "I am too old. I feel comfortable staying in the temple where I am right now." He sent the envoy away three times. Eventually, the envoy returned and pleaded with the master, "I will be beheaded if you do not come with me." Master Shanzhao said, "In that case, why don't you go back first. I will follow you shortly."

Master Shanzhao, having sent the envoy back, took a bath and asked everyone in the temple to gather for dinner. During dinner, he said, "I need to leave for a long trip. Who can come with me?" Someone on the side said he would. Then, the master asked him how far he could travel in a day. He said he could walk forty miles. The master said, "Then, you will not be able to catch up with me." Then, someone else volunteered. Master Shanzhao asked the question again, and the student's answer was, "Sixty miles." "You cannot catch up with me either," the master said. The server on the side then said, "I can catch up with you." The master was surprised and asked, "How far can you walk each day?" The server said, "When you arrive, I will be there too." The master responded and said, "Great! Then, you will certainly catch up with me!" Afterwards, the master put down his chopsticks and instantaneously achieved nirvana in his sitting position. The server on the side did the same in his standing position.

This koan is very sophisticated. It is also as uplifting as the television documentary of the astronaut's walk on the moon. However, you must ask how it pertains to your life and death and how it relates to your spiritual practice. It would be more relevant to you if you were to look at your afflictions. You have just as many afflictions as others. Because you are so burdened by afflictions, when others' afflictions come upon them, your affliction will probably also come upon you. This is a more practical thing to consider.

Even if you are unable to accomplish this kind of instantaneous nirvana, you can at least try to be a good person, as defined by the principles of benevolence, righteousness, propriety, intelligence, integrity, loyalty, filial piety, compassion, honesty and harmony. These principles value the quest for an egoless, pure mind as the basis of healthy interpersonal relationships, which are in turn characterized by human morality. When one reaches perfection in this regard, the karmic fruit of the Heavenly Realm will manifest within.

Zen teachings are very profound. However, our human perspectives are restricted by greed, anger, delusion, pride, doubt and evil desires. Therefore, our immediate assignment is to establish the basic goodness of humanity. Once we engage in practice that eliminates afflictions and habitual tendencies, we can ultimately be elevated to the realms of Buddha, Bodhisattva and the saints. I often say that thousands of rounds of meditation, scriptural studies and chanting are inferior to the transformation of a single thought. In other words, these spiritual practices have no benefit unless a person can transform his mind.

Strongly negative karma and the absence of merit will inevitably lead to an undesirable future. Each of us must live with and utilize, in the best possible way, our present karma, because it is the only basis upon which we can live and act. There is no exception. The foundation of one's spiritual practice is based on devoted effort regarding his or her current thoughts, body, environment and relationships.

Given the countless practitioners of the world, what allows you to grow and succeed? In what kind of practice do you engage to accumulate merit? This is the homework you need to accomplish: Purify yourself so that there is no space in your mind for any harmful polluted thought, jealousy, discrimination or interpersonal dispute. Let the mind be tranquil, pure and peaceful, possessing wisdom. Be compassionate, kind toward yourself and filled with altruistic intentions. If you do not do so, Buddhist lectures and koans will be

Homework ➔

no more relevant to you than storytelling.

Life is about taking responsibility for yourself. Do not think too much. Things are often very simple, but our minds tend to complicate them. The purpose of spiritual practice is to help us focus on our thoughts, actions and the transformation of our habitual tendencies. As modern-day people, being distant from the age of the saints, we must redouble our efforts in spiritual cultivation.

## Fragmentation Will Not Bring Progress

Zen Master Fayan Wenyi once studied under Master Huiling, but even after a long period of study he was not enlightened. Therefore, he decided to travel with two peer practitioners on a pilgrimage. On the way, they encountered a snowstorm and asked to stay at a Ksitigarbha hermitage, of which Master Arhat Guichen was the abbot. Master Guichen asked them, "Where are you headed?" Master Wenyi answered, "Just traveling on a pilgrimage." Master Guichen then asked, "What is the pilgrimage about?" Master Wenyi said, "I do not know." Master Guichen was pleased and said, "The unknown is the most intimate."

The three practitioners later discussed the saying, "The world and I share the same root," as introduced by Grand Master Sengzhao. This teaching suggests that the enlightened mind is as vast as the void and all-pervasive in infinite dharma realms. Its function instantly moves the entire universe because, of course, the mind and the universe are inseparable. This is how vast the mind's capacity is. Master Guichen asked, "If the world and you share the same root, are you and the world the same or different?" Master

Wenyi answered, "The same." Hearing this, Master Guichen raised two fingers. Master Wenyi saw this and said, "Different!" Master Guichen again held up two fingers and then walked away.

Master Wenyi was bewildered because he did not understand the meaning of Master Guichen's action. Eventually, the storm subsided and the three, carrying their packs, bid farewell to Master Guichen. As the master escorted them to the door, he pointed to a rock and asked, "You often say that 'the three realms are only the Mind, all phenomena is only Consciousness.' Now, tell me, is this rock inside or outside your mind?" Master Wenyi responded, "Inside the mind." Master Guichen said, "Why do you want to carry a rock in your mind as a traveling monk?" At the time, Master Wenyi, who was not yet enlightened, realized that Master Guichen was a great practitioner in dharma, so he decided to stay and learn from him.

Each day, for the first month of his stay with Master Guichen, Master Wenyi would express his enthusiasm for sharing his understanding of the dharma. However, no matter what he said the teacher would tell him, "Not so." Finally, Master Wenyi said, "I have already told you everything I know about Buddhism. So, what on earth is the truth?" Master Guichen answered, "From the perspective of the teaching, all is just as it is." Hearing this, Master Wenyi became enlightened.

The mind is already present, as are its current karma, effects and phenomena. Everything exists precisely as it is dictated to be. Master Linji once said, "If you could calm the mind that is forever pursuing thoughts, you would be no different from that old man Sakyamuni." Once you let go of all your delusions and attachments, the innate nature of the mind will emerge.

Does Master Fayan Wenyi's experience sound unreachable to you? The reality is that you have not traveled far enough as a practitioner. You do not understand what it means to share the same root with the world. Day in and day out, you neglect proper thoughts and develop various attachments in your mind, but you do not ponder what you learn. If your practice has not reached the level of Master Wenyi's, the statement, "from the perspective of the teaching, all is just as is" will not enlighten you. Consider the saying, "Familiarity breeds contempt." Because you often hear and read Zen doctrines, you begin to take them for granted and therefore underestimate the importance of dharma.

Master Wenyi eventually established his own Zen meditation hall, succeeding to the teachings of Master Arhat Guichen. Because Master Wenyi had also studied under Master Changqing Huiling for a long time, Master Changqing Huiling's lead student, Zizhao, went to visit Master Wenyi. When Zizhao arrived at the temple, he asked Master Wenyi whose teachings he espoused. Master Wenyi said, "Ksitigarbha's." In other words, he had succeeded to the teaching lineage of Master Arhat Guichen instead of Master Changqing Huiling.

Zizhao was not pleased with the answer. He said, "Isn't your behavior a betrayal to our late master?" Master Wenyi said, "I did not understand this one thing he taught." Zizhao responded immediately, "What did you not understand? You can ask now." Master Wenyi told him, "'It stands out singularly, alone among all phenomena.' What does that mean?"

Master Changqing Huiling had studied with Master Xuansha and Master Xuefeng for over twenty years. Even though he had studied and meditated so diligently that he wore through seven meditation cushions, he had not attained enlightenment. One day, his mind was awakened as he rolled up the curtain. Immediately, he said, "How ironic. How ironic. I roll up the curtain and see the world. If asked what I understood, I will shut their mouth up with a fly brush spake." Master Xuefeng was excited and told Master Xuansha that the student was at last enlightened.

Master Xuansha disagreed with him. He suspected that Master Changqin Huiling had only stumbled upon such a verse as the result of studying Zen for so long. Therefore, he must be tested again. It is true that, after studying Zen scriptures and koans for a long time, a practitioner is more or less versed in doctrines, thus making it possible to utter something profound and Zen-like without actually being enlightened. So, Master Xuefeng asked Master Changqing Huiling to describe his understanding in regard to his enlightenment. Master Changqing Huiling said, "It stands out singularly alone among all phenomena. One can only know it intimately by oneself. In the past I mistakenly seek while coming and going, now I see it as the cool ice in the fire."

Master Wenyi said he had not understood this verse when studying under Master Changqing Huiling. Hearing this, Zizhao lifted up his fly brush to illustrate the verse. Master Wenyi said, "Now, did you learn this from Master Changqing Huiling or is it your own understanding?" Zizhao was dumbfounded.

Master Wenyi continued, "'It stands out singularly, alone

among all phenomena,' so should I sweep away all phenomena or should I not do so?" Sweeping away means negation; not sweeping away means one takes responsibility. So, the question is this: Should we negate phenomena or not?" Zizhao answered, "No." Master Wenyi said, "Two." The rest of the students who were present said, "Sweep away phenomena."

The statement that "it stands out singularly, alone among all phenomena" clearly states that it stands out singularly, alone among all phenomena! The question of whether to negate phenomena or not is such that both fall into duality. Zizhao therefore realized that his spirituality had not yet reached the level of realization equal to that of Master Wenyi. Ashamed, he stood up to take leave. Master Wenyi told him, "You can repent the sins of killing your parents. However, it is even more difficult to amend the slander of great wisdom." After that, Zizhao studied under Master Wenyi.

A sage said, "Zen study must be sincerely carried out. Aspiration for enlightenment must be truly intended." It was by no means easy for Master Zizhao to become the senior monk underneath Master Changqing Huiling, but he did achieve enlightenment after all. Upon his enlightenment, however, he did not open his own school of Zen teaching.

It matters a great deal whether a person is enlightened or not. As you listen to this koan, does it feel as distant and impersonal as watching the astronauts land on the moon? It relates directly to your life, but if you cannot relate to it, it is because your spirituality has not reached a sufficient level of understanding. Similarly, all sentient beings possess the Buddha nature, but their lack of spiritual depth renders the manifestation of the innate mind far less than ideal.

Zen koans and teachings can be as fascinating as storytelling, but spiritual work is a practical matter. It comes down to two questions: Is the mind peaceful and pure? Has it foregone all attachments and troubles? If not, the scriptural principles will only become a spiritual burden or even poison. It is unrealistic to hope for a bright future if you merely enjoy the stories without applying the principles to amend your shortcomings. Practice requires genuine diligence. Spiritual growth requires calm, honest introspection.

You must become the protagonist in the story of your life as opposed to watching others' great achievements with a sense of longing. You must personally engage the practice in order to intimately savor its reward. Otherwise, all is empty talk. Spiritual enlightenment requires a solid foundation. It requires taking care of your mind, actions and thoughts so that the mind can truly come to peace. Our desire for the spiritual richness of fulfillment requires that we make very concrete progress in correcting our mistakes. Otherwise, our spiritual quest will be fragmented.

A Zen master once said, "Do not come to meditate only when the teacher is here and then go home when he leaves. These endless comings and goings will not amount to much, will they?" Scriptural studies, devotion, meditation, repentance, prayer, chanting and listening to lectures are all secondary efforts. The most important and worthwhile thing is to be able to change our thoughts, become aware of vexations and let go of attachment. Therefore, real effort lies in self-reflection and solid practice. The purity, peace and tranquility of the mind are the true measures of our spiritual practice.

The spring breeze urges the blossoming of

red, white and purple flowers.

The summer pond is decorated with

green, yellow and red lotuses.

Moon Goddess Chang-e's needlework veils

the waning of the autumn moon.

Winter snow covers the mountains with

layers of white blankets.

With one piece of clothing and one bowl for alms,

A monk travels to spread the blessings of the Way

through all four seasons.

An enlightened one returns to the root of being,

as he understands the mind and embraces his innate nature.

In such a state, traveling the world is

a matter of snapping a finger.

# GLOSSARY

# GLOSSARY

**AMIDA BUDDHA:** The Amida Buddha, also known as Amitabha Buddha or Amitayus Buddha, is the root teacher of the Western Land of Bliss. Amida means infinity. Amitabha and Amitayus mean infinite light (space) and infinite life (time), respectively.

**AMITABHA SUTRA:** Scriptural text that describes the aspirations and miraculous manifestations of the Western Land of Bliss of Amitabha Buddha, which is also known as Amida Buddha.

**VENERABLE ANANDA:** Venerable Ananda is the Buddha's cousin and attendant. Among the ten chief disciples of the Buddha, Ananda is known for having attended the most teachings and for his remarkable memory of the spoken words of the Buddha. He is well respected and remembered for his gentle nature, eagerness to be of help and great empathy with others' suffering. He often requests teachings from the Buddha on behalf of others, and was instrumental in the establishment of the order of nuns. Venerable Ananda is also the Third Patriarch of Zen, starting with the historical Buddha.

**ARAHANT:** One who has attained a spiritual state of liberation in which habitual tendencies, such as defining and clinging to the notion of "I," have been purified to the point that the individual is free from life after life of reincarnation.

**ARAHANTSHIP:** Arahantship is the spiritual state in which an arahant dwells.

**ATTACHMENT:** Attachment is a state of mind characterized by grasping or holding onto mental functions such as thoughts, feelings and perceptions. The most fundamental attachment human beings have is to their sense of an independent selfhood.

**MASTER BAI-YUN SHO-DUAN (ALSO WHITE CLOUD ZEN MASTER) (1025 - 72):** Master Bai-Yun is of the Linji lineage; the forty-sixth generation in Zen from the historical Buddha. One day his teacher Master Yang-Qi asked whether he remembered the poem of enlightenment of his master of ordination. In response, Bai-Yun recited it: "I possess a lustrous pearl / locked and concealed by dust and burden / now that the dust has cleared away and the light shines through / illuminating the ten thousand mountains and rivers." Upon hearing this, Master

Yang-Qi jumped up and laughed out loud. Bai-Yun was dumbfounded and could not sleep for the whole night. The next day, Master Yang-Qi asked, "Did you witness the exorcism yesterday?" (This conversation is reenacted during the time of year when there are staged dramas among the lay people for the purpose of expelling evil spirits.) Bai-Yun said, "Yes." Yang-Qi said, "You can't match up to it." Bai-Yun asked, "What do you mean?" Yang-Qi said, "It loves people's laughter, while you fear people's laughter." Upon hearing this, Master Bai-Yun attained enlightenment.

**MASTER BAIZHANG:** Master Baizhang Huai-Hai (720 - 814), the teacher of Huang-Bo, was instrumental in reforming and establishing the rules that governed how Zen practitioners should live and practice together as a self-sustaining community where, in addition to meditation, manual labor for farming and the upkeep of the monastery became an integral part of Zen practice. The event that was the precursor to his enlightenment went like this: Once, as he attended to Master Ma-tzu, a flock of wild ducks flew by. Ma-tzu asked him, "What is it?" Baizhang replied, "Wild ducks." Ma-tzu then asked, "Where did it go?" Baizhang said, "They flew away." Without warning, Ma-tzu turned around and got a hold of Baizhang's nose and twisted hard. Baizhang cried out in pain, and Ma-tzu said, "And you told me they flew away!?" At this instant, Baizhang had a realization. Returning to his quarters, Baizhang began to cry, and a fellow monk asked him, "Are you missing your folks?" "No." "Were you scolded by the teacher?" "No." "Then, why are you crying?" Baizhang said, "My nose was twisted by Master, and the pain didn't quite penetrate!" The other monk then asked, "What is not working out?" Baizhang said, "Go ask the master himself." When the monk asked the master about the situation, Ma-tzu said, "He [Baizhang] knows it, go ask him!" When the monk returned, Baizhang was laughing out loud! Puzzled, he said, "Baizhang, you were just crying, so why are you now laughing so hard?" Baizhang said, "Was just crying, now laughing." The monk was still puzzled. Later on Baizhang achieved a further breakthrough and his realization was confirmed by Ma-tzu.

**BARDO:** The transitional state between successive incarnation, typically in reference to what occurs after the death of the physical body but before the being takes rebirth in the one of the six possible realms.

**BODHI:** Bodhi is a Sanskrit word for awakening.

**BODHI TAO:** Tao is Chinese meaning "the Way." Bodhi Tao means the path of awakening or it refers to the principle of how the Mind functions.

**BODHI TREE:** The Bodhi Tree is the sacred fig tree in Bodh Gaya, India, under which the historical Buddha attained enlightenment.

**BODIDHARMA:** Believed to have died sometime near 536 A.D., Bodhidharma is considered the First Patriarch of Zen in China and the twenty-eighth embodiment of enlightenment since the historical Buddha. An Indian monk, Bodhidharma traveled to China to spread the teaching by focusing on the essence of dharma and freeing people from the traps of religious dogmatism. He meditated for nine years in seclusion, facing the wall in a cave near the Shao-Lin temple (often regarded as the birthplace of kung-fu) until he met Hui-Ke, who attained realization of the truth through Bodhidharma's instruction and became the Second Patriarch. In Zen, the transmission of the teaching is made directly from mind to mind; the disciple's realization is verified not by intellectual judgment or understanding but by confirmation through the teacher's intuitive evaluation. Because the essence of the dharma is beyond intellectual reasoning, only those who have directly realized the truth may assess and confirm a student's attainment. The analogy often given is that only a person who has drunk the water truly knows its taste; therefore, only the teacher is able to assess whether a student has also tasted the elixir of the true dharma. The tradition of the Zen lineage in China starts with Bodhidharma's transmission to Hui-Ke, and it continues to the Sixth Patriarch Huineng, whose revolutionizing of the Zen teaching led to the creation of the five schools of Zen Buddhism. One of several recorded teachings attributed to Bodhidharma is the Treatise on the Two Entrances and Four Practices, a short teaching that describes two approaches and four practice methods leading to spiritual realization.

**BODHISATTVA:** A *bodhisattva* is a practitioner (either in the process of attaining or having already attained a high level of spiritual awakening and freedom from suffering) who strives to help others to achieve the same state. This altruistic action is based on the profound recognition of the inseparability of the personal self from others. The term *bodhisattva* also represents the myriad pure functions that arise from the pure mind.

**BUDDHA DHARMA:** The teaching of the Buddha.

**BUDDHAHOOD:** Buddhahood is the spiritual state of complete liberation from suffering and the perfection of all virtues. It is the state of complete realization of the essence of the Mind and the perfection of the Mind's functions.

**BUDDHA NATURE:** The fundamental nature of the Mind that is innate in all beings. Because of this fundamental equality in the nature of the Mind, all beings have the potential for awakening.

**CAOXI:** A river in southern China where the Zen teaching of the Sixth Patriarch began. Therefore, Caoxi also refers to the Zen lineage and teaching that can be traced to the Sixth Patriarch.

**COLLECTIVE (THE):** A reference to the totality of all manifestations of the Mind.

**CONFUCIANISM:** A set of ethical doctrines preached by Confucius (551 - 478 B.C.E.) that has been highly influential in China. Confucianism stresses the importance of proper conduct and responsibility in the context of relationships, such as the relationship between rulers and the ruled, father and son, husband and wife, elders and the young, and between friends. It is a humanistic ethical system not based on any theistic belief.

**CHAO-CHOU ("JOSHU" IN JAPANESE):** One of the most famous Chinese Zen masters of the Tang Dynasty (618 - 907 A.D.), Chao-Chou is widely known for the classic koan where, in response to the question of whether a dog possesses the Buddha Nature (i.e. the potential for awakening) he uttered the word "wu" (or "mu" in Japanese), which was subsequently incorporated into the practice of Zen inquiry.

**MASTER DA'AN:** Master Da'an (? - 883) took his monastic vow in Mt. Huang-Bo and, for several years, studied the monastic code of discipline. Yearning for the highest teaching, he left and met Master Baizhang, ultimately attaining enlightenment. He once addressed an assembly of monks: "Since you are all here, just settle down. What is there to seek? If you seek to be the Buddha, you are already the Buddha! Why keep wandering around others' houses, restless like a thirsty deer under a scorching sun! How can you ever find what you seek this way?"

**MASTER DA-HUI:** Master Da-Hui (1089 - 1163) was the best-known advocate of the hua-tou practice, which is the continuous and intensive questioning of a koan as crystallized in a single word such as "wu" (or "mu" in Japanese) or in the question, "What is the meaning of Bodhidharma's coming from the West?" or "Who is the one reciting the Buddha's name?" The purpose of the hua-tou practice is to utilize the doubt generated by the questioning to penetrate our habitual attachments and directly experience the nature of the pure mind.

**DAO (OR TAO):** Also referred to as "the Way," it refers to the principle that governs the functioning of the Mind and reality.

**DAOISM (OR TAOISM):** Taoism is a set of philosophical teachings and religious practices that originated in China and became an organized religion in the fifth century A.D. The key text in Taoism is the *Tao Te Ching* by Lao-Tzu. Taoists believe that man should live in harmony with nature through the Tao or "the Way," as the idea of a great cosmic harmony. Taoist beliefs emphasize self-refinement, liberty and the pursuit of immortality.

**DA-YU:** A mountain in southern China where the Sixth Patriarch gave this first teaching to a spiritual seeker after attaining enlightenment.

**DEVA:** A non-human being who possesses greater power and whose mind strongly exhibits the qualities of kindness, compassion, sympathetic joy and equanimity.

**DHARMA:** *Dharma* literally means law, rule or duty. It may refer to the Buddhist teaching or to the ultimate truth as expressed by the teaching. In Buddhist philosophy, the term *dharma* is also used in reference to phenomenon.

**DHARMAKAYA:** *Dharmakaya*, literally "truth body" in Sanskrit, constitutes the primordial essence of the Mind out of which all phenomena arise.

**DIAMOND SUTRA:** A Mahayana sutra based on a dialogue between the Buddha and his disciple Subhuti, it focuses on the practice of overcoming dualism and attachment to forms.

**DUALISM:** Concepts characterized by opposites of mutually dependent parts such as subject and object, self and others, good and evil, etc.

**EGOLESSNESS:** One of the central teachings of the Buddha, it points out the illusion of "I" or ego identification.

**EMPTINESS:** A reference to the lack of intrinsic existence of any phenomenon.

**ENLIGHTENMENT:** The recognition of the nature of the Mind.

**ESOTERIC:** See Vajrayana.

**FA-HUA REALM:** The state of Buddhahood as expressed in the Fa-hua Sutra.

**FIVE AGGREGATES:** The aspects that comprise our experiential reality: matter (or form), feeling, perception, volition (or mental constructs) and consciousness.

**FIVE COMMANDMENTS AND THE TEN GOOD ACTIONS:** The five precepts of a lay Buddhist practitioner: no killing, no stealing, no wrongful sexual conduct, no falsehood in speech, no intoxicant. The ten good actions are typically stated as negations: no killing, no stealing, no wrongful sexual conduct, no abusive speech, no seductive speech, no divisive speech, no lies, no greed, no hatred, no delusion.

**FOUR ELEMENTS:** The four elements are earth, water, fire and wind, but more specifically they refer to the qualities of solidity, fluidity, heat and motion as possessed by material phenomena.

**FOUR NOBLE TRUTHS:** Comprised in the first sermon given by the historical Buddha, the Four Noble Truths are: (1) the nature of suffering; (2) the cause of suffering is attachment; (3) suffering ceases when attachment is removed; and (4) the way to remove attachment is through the proper cultivation of eight aspects of life: understanding (or view) of reality, thought, speech, action, livelihood, effort, attention and mental concentration.

**FOURTH PATRIARCH OF ZEN:** Zen patriarchs are considered the orthodox line of transmission of Zen teaching; the embodiment of the direct realization of the truth as opposed to mere intellectual understanding or written words. In China, Daoxin (580 - 651 A.D.) is recognized as the Fourth Patriarch based on his attainment of this direct realization of the truth.

**GOLDEN OX:** A Zen master famous for laughing while calling the monks to take their meals. Other Zen masters of the past who deployed unusual means of teaching include Chao-Chou (Joshu), who is known for his tea offering to visiting practitioners; Yunmen, known for his cakes; and Linji, who used a sudden shout to effect a breakthrough in the student's realization.

**HINAYANA:** The "lesser vehicle" in contrast to Mahayana, the "great vehicle." The concept is an attempt to distinguish the one whose spiritual practice is primarily focused on personal liberation from the one whose practice is motivated by the ultimate liberation of all beings.

**HEART SUTRA:** A short text in which Avalokiteshvara, the Bodhisattva of Compassion, described the non-dualistic nature of reality through a series of negations. It states that form and emptiness are the inseparable aspects of all existence. This realization is the ultimate wisdom that will remove the fundamental ignorance from which all suffering stems.

**HUA-TOU PRACTICE:** The continuous, intensive questioning of a Zen story as crystallized by a single word such as "wu" (or "mu" in Japanese) or a phrase such as, "What is the meaning of Bodhidharma's coming from the West?" or "Who is the one reciting the Buddha's name?" The purpose of the hua-tou practice is to utilize the doubt generated by the questioning to penetrate our habitual attachments so that we can directly experience the nature of the pure mind.

**HUAYEN:** In Chinese, *hua-yen* means flower garlands. In that country, a school of Buddhism emerged in the sixth century based on the teaching of the Flower Garland Sutra.

**MASTER HUANG-BO:** Zen Master Huang-Bo (or Huang-Po) (776 - 856 A.D.) was the teacher of Master Linji, widely known for his directness in pointing out the One Mind, which exists beyond language and form. Huang-Bo is the name of the mountain where he taught. (It is customary in China to refer to a Zen master by his place of residence.) Teaching on the emptiness of the mind, he said: "Ordinary beings focus on situation, but the practitioners of the Way focus on the mind; to forget both mind and situation is the real dharma. To forget the situation is relatively easy, in comparison to the utmost difficulty of the task of forgetting the mind. Men are afraid to forget the mind because they fear the emptiness, where there is nothing to hold on; they do not realize that true emptiness is not nothingness, it is simply the realm of One Truth."

**MASTER HUINENG:** Sixth Patriarch Huineng (638 - 713 B.C.E.), regarded as the most important figure in Zen Buddhism, was instrumental in the wide propagation of Zen practice in China and later in Japan and Korea. All five schools of Zen Buddhism can trace their lineage to Huineng. His teaching, as recorded in the Platform Sutra, is the most important source of early Zen teaching.

**JADE EMPEROR:** The ruler of the heavenly immortal beings, according to the mythology of Daoism.

**KARMA:** Karma means action. It also refers to the result of action, since the spiritual law of cause and effect states that the result is always preceded by causal action. Karma is sometimes misunderstood as a kind of fatalism, but the ultimate cause of all phenomena is the Mind, so mastery of the Mind ensures mastery over karma.

**KOAN:** A koan is literally a public case or a record of Zen dialogue. These dialogues are often used as means to test a student's realization. Such dialogues can seem absurd, illogical or trivial; they can generate a sense of bewilderment or doubt in the student's mind, which can only be resolved by transcending conventional thought and attachment.

**LAND OF BLISS:** The same as Pure Land.

**LAO TZU:** The founder of Daoism (or Taoism).

**LAW OF CREATION:** The principle concerning the manifestation of phenomena.

**LAYMAN FU:** Fu Shan-Hui (497 - 569), a contemporary of Bodhidharma, was highly regarded for his spiritual attainment. His "Mind King" writing is a classic of Zen study. In Buddhism, there are many examples of lay practitioners who have exceptionally high spiritual attainment. Another famous example is Vimalakirti, a layman whose teachings to the chief disciples of the Buddha and many bodhisattvas are recorded in the Vimalakirti Nirdesa Sutra. This respect for lay practitioners demonstrates the essential idea in Buddhism that all beings possess the Buddha nature, or the potential for awakening. Regardless of external form, the essence of all beings and the Buddhas is the same.

**MASTER LINJI:** Zen Master Linji (787 - 867) founded the Linji school of Zen, five generations after the Sixth Patriarch Huineng. Linji approached his teacher, Master Huang-Bo, three times to ask for the true meaning of Buddha dharma. Each time, before he could even finish his question, he was hit by Huang-Bo. Discouraged, he took leave and went to Master Da-Yu, whereupon he related his encounter. Da-Yu told him that Huang-Bo did it out of his motherly heart of kindness. Upon hearing this, Linji attained awakening and commented that Huang-Bo's teaching was not so great! Well known for his rigorous, intensive style of teaching, Master Linji utilized the so-called four shouts and eight staffs as means for breaking his students' attachments, certainly as an expression of the influence of his own awakening experience. The Linji school of Zen, also known as Rinzai in Japanese, is one of the five schools of Zen that originated in ancient China and is most representative of Zen practice today. The Linji school of Zen is characterized by its intensity of practice and the use of a shout or a staff as a means of lighting the spark of realization within the practitioner. Today, there remain only the Linji school and Caodong (or "Soto" in Japanese) schools of Zen.

**MAHAMUDRA (OR GREAT SOUL):** A school of Tibetan Buddhism. The name implies that all existence is sealed with the essence of the absolute.

**MAHAYANA:** One of the major schools Buddhism; *Mahayana* literally means "great vehicle." Central to the Mahayana teaching is the concept of the bodhisattva, for whom altruism is a key aspect of the spiritual path, being motivated by selfless compassion arising from the realization of the essential inseparability between himself and others. While other schools of Buddhism may not emphasize the ideal of a bodhisattva path, it should be recognized that each path manifests according to the karma of the individual practitioner, just as different illnesses require unique medicines to effect their cures. Practices that seem focused on liberating the practitioner's suffering can also contribute significantly to the well-being of others. The merit of any path should only be judged within the context of the practitioner's unique situation in terms of its suitability to guide that individual toward the realization of the Universal Truth.

**MAITREYA:** The next Buddha who will appear in our world. In Zen, Maitreya represents the Mind's pure function in the present moment.

**MANDALA:** A visualization of the universe, a mandala is an idealized environment that symbolizes the manifestation of the pure mind.

**MANTRA:** A sacred sound, either one syllable in a word or a set of words that have spiritual or mystical power. A mantra can have the power to protect, purify, eliminate or magnify certain states of consciousness as well as the power to generate other effects. This power comes from the pure function of the Mind, which is evoked through repetition of the mantra.

**MERIT:** Often considered to be the "positive force" that leads to desirable results in our life experience; more specifically, it is the difference in the reality manifested by the mind due to an elevated spiritual state of attainment.

**MIND DHARMA:** Mind dharma is the aspect of Buddhist teaching that directly addresses the nature of the Mind.

**MIND GROUND:** The Mind can be described in terms of its essence, form and functions; thus the term "mind ground" refers to the "essence" aspect of the Mind.

**MIND KING:** Because all functions of the mind—such as perception, feeling and consciousness—arise from the Mind, it is regarded as the king or the governing essence of all functions. The term "Mind King" appeared in a hymn written by the Third Patriarch Seng-Ts'an, who lived in the sixth century A.D. It is also the name of a hymn, attributed to Layman Fu, that is a classic in Zen study.

**MONKEY KING:** The main character in the Chinese classic novel *Journey to the West.* In the story, the monkey king rules the Mount Flower and Fruit but becomes the disciple of a great Buddhist master (see Tang Sanzang) who vows to make the treacherous trip to India on foot in order to bring back more scriptures. While the story can be read as a magical fantasy, it can also be understood as a parable for the way the mind works. The monkey king represents the restless aspect of the mind, or the "monkey mind," of an unenlightened being. One of the powers of the monkey king is his ability to manifest seventy-two transformations, thus symbolizing the quick, flexible and creative nature of the mind.

**NIRMANAKAYA:** The moment-to-moment manifestation of phenomena from the Mind, it often refers specifically to the manifestation of the Buddha's physical presence from the essence of the Mind.

**NIRVANA:** An eternal state of liberation, where the suffering of birth and death ends on the gross level of the physical body, or on the subtle level of the moment-to-moment manifestation and disappearance of phenomena. Liberation from birth and death does not negate the nature of phenomena. Instead, it frees the practitioner from attachment to phenomena as something permanent, so that the changing nature of phenomena no longer causes fundamental struggle or suffering within.

**ONE COMPOSITE:** The physical world is "one composite," because it is an entity that emerges through the composition of many elements. Our physical-psychological being is also described as one composite, as it is a collection of physical and psychological phenomena: the physical form (body), feelings, perceptions, volitions and consciousness.

**PARINIRVANA:** The state of nirvana upon the death of the physical body of an enlightened being. It symbolizes the complete purification of all traces of impure karma. Alternatively, parinirvana can be understood as a state of liberation in which the function of the mind is completely pure.

**PLATFORM SUTRA:** A sutra containing a recorded biography and account of the life and teaching of the Sixth Patriarch Huineng. The title of this book is based on the opening verse of the sutra: "The Awakened Self Nature / Primordially pure it is /Just use this Mind / Directly actualize Buddhahood." This sutra contains the wisdom and essence of early Zen teaching in China. When it was written, its highly accessible language pointed out the formless truth that underlies all existence, dispelled many common misunderstandings of classical scripture, and revealed the purpose behind various forms of popular religious practices. This sutra remains highly relevant to modern society, as spiritual seekers attempt to cut through various presentations and discover the real message.

**POET BAI (OR LI BAI):** Li Bai (701 - 762 A.D.) is considered one of the greatest poets in Chinese history. His works are characterized by the spontaneity and influence of Taoism and Zen. He has also been called the Poet Transcendent or the Retired Scholar of Azure Lotus. One of his most famous poems, "Drinking Along Under Moonlight," has been translated into English.

**PRIMORDIAL MIND:** Pure Mind or Innate Mind. It refers to the uncontaminated, unobstructed nature of the Mind, which is the origin and source of all existence.

**PURE LAND:** The pure living environment manifested by a Buddha through the pure function of the Mind. The power of his vows makes each Buddha's pure land unique in its characteristics and the manifestation of an idealized environment for facilitating his spiritual practice. Practitioners of Pure Land Buddhism purify their minds and vow to take rebirth after death in Buddha's pure land in order to further their spiritual practice. Because the mind and our physical environment are inseparable aspects of the same essence, the practice of Pure Land is essentially the practice of purifying the mind.

**REALM OF FLOWER ADORNMENT:** See Huayen.

**SAKYAMUNI:** Sakya, or Shakya, is the Buddha's clan of origin in northern India, near the foothills of the Himalayas in present-day Nepal. The historical Buddha, known as Sakyamuni ("Sage of the Sakya") Buddha (563 - 483 B.C.E.), was born a prince. He abandoned a life of wealth, power and luxury in order to pursue a spiritual journey on which he sought to resolve the problems of the inevitable suffering of birth, death, illness and aging that he observed when venturing outside the protective environment of his palace.

**SAMADHI:** A general term referring to a very high level of meditative concentration characterized by a profound degree of mental calm and clarity of awareness; depending on the context, it can also refer to the state of non-dual consciousness where the distinction of subject versus object is dissolved.

**SAMSARA:** The cycles of birth, death and rebirth in the world of appearance. In Buddhist cosmology, samsara is described as six different states of existence determined by a person's accumulated habitual tendencies and dominant karma. The six realms are: heavenly being, human, jealous god, hungry ghost, animal and hell being. Rebirth as a heavenly being is due to a predominance of compassion, loving kindness, sympathetic joy, and equanimity in consciousness and actions. Rebirth as a jealous god occurs due to causes such as charitable actions conducted with regret or impure motivations that lead to material abundance but strong dissatisfaction and jealousy. Existence as a human being is the result of positive and negative thoughts, speech and actions, none of which is very strong. The hungry ghost is characterized by greed and craving; the animal realm is dominated by a lack of awareness and delusion; and reincarnation as a hell being is caused by negative afflictions, including anger or actions (such as killing) carried out with strong intent and accumulated force. Samsara can also be understood as a metaphor of our moment-to-moment consciousness. The moment a person gives rise to compassion in the mind, that individual manifests the heavenly being's existence on earth. The next moment, the arising of greed can manifest the state of a hungry ghost. From this perspective, rebirth in a different realm does not merely occur after physical death but is instead the moment-to-moment manifestation of the mind's function.

**SANGHA:** A term that often refers to the monastic community but also includes the community of lay and monastic Buddhist practitioners. The sangha is significant because, without those who actually practice, teach and embody the wisdom and compassion of the teaching in their daily lives, the real benefit and goal of the teaching cannot be fulfilled.

**SEAL OF DHARMA:** A reference to the characteristics of phenomena: impermanence, non-self and suffering. Sometimes a fourth aspect is added, which states that nirvana is true peace. The term *nirvana* refers to the essence of all existence that is beyond conditionality and not subject to birth and death.

**SENTIENT BEING:** In Buddhism, any being that is able to have a conscious experience of feelings and perception.

**SHEN XIU:** A contemporary of the Sixth Patriarch Huineng and the leading disciple of the Fifth Patriarch. To demonstrate his understanding to the Fifth Patriarch, he composed the following verse:

> The body is a Bodhi tree,
> The mind is a clear standing mirror.
> Diligently and constantly we shall polish it,
> Let not a single dust settle.

In response the Sixth Patriarch, an illiterate laborer in the monastery who had never attended even one teaching by the Fifth Patriarch, uttered this verse:

> Bodhi has no tree in essence,
> A clear mirror is not a stand either.
> Since the beginning there was not a single thing,
> From where could any dust come?

Huineng's verse demonstrated profound insight into the formless essence of reality, but Shen Xiu's verse is still great advice for all spiritual practitioners. Through diligent practice, Shen Xiu later attained enlightenment as well. Because the Sixth Patriarch moved to southern China to spread his teaching while Shen Xiu moved to the North, people sometimes refer to Huineng's teaching as the Southern School and Shen Xiu's teaching as the Northern School.

**SIX BODHISATTVA PRACTICES:** These are generosity, morality, patience, effort, concentration and wisdom.

**SIXTH PATRIARCH:** The Sixth Patriarch Huineng (638 - 713 B.C.E.), regarded as the most important figure in Zen Buddhism, was instrumental in the wide propagation of Zen practice in China and later in Japan and Korea. All five schools of Zen Buddhism can trace their lineage to Huineng. His teaching, as recorded in the Platform Sutra, is the most important source of early Zen teaching.

**SURRANGAMA REALM:** The state of Buddhahood as expressed in the Surrangama Sutra.

**SURRANGAMA SUTRA:** A sutra that describes the philosophy and practice for attaining the surrangama samadhi, a state of complete enlightenment. The sutra begins with Ananda, the Buddha's attendant, being rescued from the verge of losing his monastic vows to sensual temptations and followed by subsequent teachings in which the Buddha guided Ananda in search of his true self. Also well known in the text is a chapter in which twenty-four bodhisattvas describe different methods of practice and how they realize their true nature. Additionally, the sutra contains descriptions of fifty deviant states of mind that a spiritual practitioner may encounter, and the Surrangama Mantra, which is recited as part of regular morning service by all sects of the Mahayana tradition in China.

**SUTRA:** Sutra are Buddhist scriptures that contain teachings of the Buddha.

**TATHAGATA:** A Sanskrit term frequently used by the Buddha in reference to himself, literally meaning "he who has come as he has gone." The term can also be understood as the two aspects of the Mind, the "essence" aspect, which is the source and refuge of all phenomena, and the "function" aspect, which is the presentation of reality.

**TEN DIRECTIONS:** The "ten directions (of space)" is a Buddhist cosmological concept comprising the north, south, east, west, up, down, northwest, northeast, southeast and southwest.

**THERAVADA:** Literally, "teaching of the elder," Theravada is the oldest school of Buddhism. It is now practiced mainly in Sri Lanka and Southeast Asia.

**THIRD PATRIARCH SENG-CAN (XUN-CAN, SENG-TSAN):** The Third Patriarch of Zen, who lived in the sixth century A.D., to whom the poem "Faith in Mind" has been attributed. This poem has been quoted extensively by past and present Zen masters in their teachings and writings. The poem begins:

> The ultimate Way is not difficult at all,
> Except your picking and choosing.
> Just stop craving and hatred,
> Then you will thoroughly understand.

**THREE INSIGHTS OF ONE MIND (RELEVANT TO DUALITY):** A concept in which *emptiness, dependent designation* (for example the conceptual labeling given to phenomena) and *the middle way* are the three aspects of non-duality, and therefore the complete penetration into non-duality through any one aspect will necessarily bring about the realization of the other aspects of non-duality. Thus it is actually not possible to realize any aspect of non-duality apart from the others.

**TIBETAN BUDDHISM:** The form of Buddhism practiced in Tibet. As Buddhism spread throughout Asia, it incorporated elements of indigenous religions as a skillful means of spreading the same spiritual message of the Buddha. Therefore, the customs and rituals of Tibetan Buddhism share similarities with the Bon religion. Tibetan Buddhism is also categorized as Vajrayana (the Diamond Vehicle), which incorporates the principles and practice of Tantra, which means bringing awareness to that which is deluded. However, Vajrayana teaching originated in India and is also practiced in China and Japan in various forms. One unique aspect of Tibetan Buddhism is the explicit identification of young children as reincarnated teachers or accomplished masters. These special individuals, referred to as *tulkus,* are given systematic, rigorous religious training in order to ensure the continuation of spiritual teaching and practices. The most prominent example is the current Dalai Lama, who is the fourteenth reincarnation of the same spiritual being who has been given the training and role as a religious leader for the Tibetan people in general.

**TRIPLE JEWELS:** The Triple Jewels—namely the Buddha, the dharma and the sangha—are the points of refuge in Buddhism. In the literal sense, the term *Buddha* refers to the historical Buddha, who left us with the dharma (or

Intrinsic Awakened Nature

teaching), and the sangha represents the community of practitioners who apply the teaching in their practice and propagate the teaching to others. The Buddha, dharma and sangha also represent the awakening nature of the Mind, the universal principle that governs the manifestation of the Mind, and the pure functioning of the Mind. Because they represent the keys to liberation from all suffering as well as the attainment of eternal peace and joy, they are considered the most precious entities in this world and are referred to as jewels. By taking refuge in the Triple Jewels, the practitioner accepts these three points of refuge as the ultimate guide in his spiritual life.

**TWELVE LINKS OF DEPENDENT ORIGINATION (PRATITYASAMUTPADA):** A Buddhist teaching that describes a series of causes and effects that lead to our suffering, the reversal of which leads to liberation from suffering. It begins by stating ignorance as a causal condition that leads to the arising of mental formations. These mental formations, as causal conditions, then lead to (dualistic) consciousness. Consciousness, as a causal condition, leads to mind-and-matter. In this way, each effect serves as a cause that leads to the next effect, thus constituting the chain of birth and death. Mind-and-matter is followed by sense faculties, contact, feeling, craving, clinging, becoming, birth, and aging and death. The essential point of the teaching is to show us how to transform this chain of cause and effect through spiritual practice and thereby attain liberation from suffering. If we can remove ignorance, the mental formation will cease; the cessation of mental formation means we will transcend the duality of consciousness and the object of consciousness. Having transcended that duality, we will not separate the mind from matter (another form of duality) but will ultimately achieve the resolution of all dualities. It is also possible to interrupt this chain of suffering by dissolving our craving and clinging to feelings as a habit that leads to birth and death. However, without purifying the source of duality our freedom is not complete and we are subject to future suffering. Ultimately, only by removing the ignorance of our essential nature can we attain lasting purification and freedom.

**TUSITA HEAVEN:** A celestial plane of existence where a bodhisattva is reborn before appearing in this world as Buddha.

**VAIROCANA:** The Vairocana Buddha is a historical Buddha whose name means "that which illuminates everything." This term and "Buddha" refer to emptiness or the essence of the Mind.

**VAJRAYANA:** The Diamond Vehicle, also known as Tantric Buddhism. It is an extension of Mahayana Buddhism and is similar in philosophical aspects, but because it incorporates additional esoteric techniques to achieve enlightenment, some practices can only be transmitted in person by a qualified spiritual teacher under prescribed conditions.

**VEXATION:** Mental suffering that arises due to the gap between reality; specifically, our subjective perception of such suffering.

**WESTERN LAND OF BLISS:** The pure land of Amida Buddha. According to the sutra, Amida Buddha has forty-eight great vows that create an ideal learning environment for spiritual practitioners. Among these many marvelous wonders are the ability to attend the teaching given directly by Amida Buddha and travel to the innumerable worlds of the Buddhas to receive teachings; trees and birds, whose sounds and sights give dharma teaching without spoken words; and having an unlimited life span in which to deepen spiritual practice. Through the empowerment of Amida Buddha, a practitioner is able to take rebirth in other worlds for the sake of learning or helping other beings without the danger of regression to pitiful states of suffering and ignorance. This pure land is so wonderful and free of all unpleasant aspects of worldly existence that it is also referred to as the Land of Bliss.

**MASTER WU-MEN:** Master Wu-Men (1183 - 1260) is famous for having compiled the *Gateless Barrier,* a collection of koans, together with his commentaries. He attained enlightenment by engaging the hua-tou "wu" (see Chao-Chou), and therefore he is known as "Wu-Men," which literally means "no door (or gate)" or the door (or gate) of "wu."

**MASTER XIAN-YAN:** In order to awaken the potential in him, Master Xian-Yan's teacher once asked him, "I am not interested in what you have learned or remembered from books and studies. Before you were born, before you distinguish what is east and west, from that place of your original self, now try to tell me something." Xian-Yan remained speechless for a long time. He then offered some words about his understanding of the Way, but the teacher disapproved of everything he said. Xian-Yan said to his teacher, "Please explain the Way to me." His teacher answered, "What I can say is my own understanding. What benefit is there to flash it in front of your eyes?" Xian-Yan then returned to his quarters. Having poured through all the books and found nothing with which he could respond to the teacher, he said to himself, "Hunger cannot be satisfied by drawing a cake." He burned up all the notes and books and said, "I shall forget about Buddhism for my whole life and simply be a traveling monk and rest the mind."

**WEI TUO:** A protective deity of a Buddhist monastery, in the Mahayana tradition. Wei Tuo Bodhisattva has vowed to protect the mind of spiritual practitioners from temptation and to maintain harmony among the sangha.

**WESTERN PARADISE:** A general reference to the Pure Land of Amida Buddha.

**POET XU DONG-PO:** (Su Dong-Po or Su-Shi) (1037 - 1101) was a major poet, artist and calligrapher of the Song Dynasty. Having passed the civil service examination at the highest degree at the age of nineteen, he began a political career. Su was demoted and exiled several times due to his philosophical differences with the policies of the central government, but he was loved and respected by the people.